MW00788931

Sanctuary:

Raw Confessions
of One of
God's Imperfect Servants

Harry Schenkel

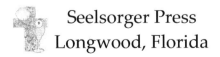

Seelsorger Press
Longwood, Florida

Sanctuary: Raw Confessions of One of God's Imperfect Servants

Copyright © 2024 Harry Schenkel

All rights reserved.

No part of this book may be reproduced in any form or by any electronic mechanical means including information storage and retrieval systems without written permission in writing from the publisher, except by a reviewer who may quote brief passages in a review.

ISBN: 979-8-9912268-0-6
ISBN: 979-8-9912268-1-3 (ebook)
ISBN: 979-8-9912268-2-0 (audiobook)

Library of Congress Control Number: 2024915592

Cover art by Lisa Schenkel

For information contact:
Seelsorger Press
Longwood, FL
info@seelsorgerpress.com

First Edition 2024

10 9 8 7 6 5 4 3 2 1
Manufactured and Printed in the United States of America

Scripture quotations labeled NRSV are New Revised Standard Version Bible, copyright © 1989 National Council of the Churches of Christ in the United States of America. Used by permission. All rights reserved worldwide.

Dictionary definitions are taken from Merriam-Webster. (n.d.). Merriam-Webster.com dictionary. Retrieved June 30, 2021, from https://www.merriam-webster.com/dictionary/stereotypy.

DEDICATION

To Lisa, Harrison, Samantha, Mackenzie, and Hunter.

You all have helped me deeper understand love and grace.

Prologue

I sat in my big-backed pastor's chair to the left of the altar, having just delivered my sermon. The chair was over a hundred years old. It had three points at the top, which made it look like something a king in the Middle Ages would have used, like a royal throne where all would come and kiss the ring of their leader. All of the pastors who had served and preached at this seaside community church on the south shore of Long Island during her 111-year history had sat in this chair when they finished their Easter Sunday sermon.

But on this Easter Sunday 2008, I was not feeling worthy of sitting in that chair. This Easter Sunday was out of whack in so many different ways. It was one of the earliest Easter Sundays that the calendar would allow, falling on March 23. Easter Sunday would not be this early again for another 153 years. But this Sunday was out of whack for me for entirely different reasons.

I just finished preaching a sermon entitled "Shake, Rattle, and Roll." Using the imagery of the angel sitting on the stone from the tomb that had been rolled away, I launched into a sermon talking about how we all move through life making our plans and thinking about things other than the importance of the empty tomb of Easter Sunday until our lives are shaken and rattled by the rude interruptions of unwelcome hardships, tragedies, and challenges, brought about by this sin-filled, broken world.

Though Easter Sunday is all about hope and victory represented in the angel sitting on top of the stone that had covered the tomb where the body of Jesus lay, and though I

5

finished that sermon pointing to the hope and victory that is ours in Christ, my personal thoughts and life were feeling more like Good Friday, with its darkness and defeat, rather than the hope, joy, and new life, that Easter Sunday is all about.

As I preached on that Easter Sunday, I pointed to how lives are shaken and rattled by many things including this exact quote from that sermon: "Our lives are often shaken when personal relationships are not what they were and falling apart ..." That line was taken directly from my own personal life. As I sat there looking out over the flock I had shepherded for over ten years now ... as I looked into the faces of so many I had helped, and prayed with, and cried with, and heard their deepest darkest sins, struggles, and fears, I was sitting there feeling like a fraud, hiding my inner decay, knowing that in the next few days and weeks my life, my family, and my ministry, were about to implode.

Since I was a teenager, a life journeying to and serving in the ministry is all I ever knew. I first felt called to service in the church during high school. By the time I set off for college, I decided that I wanted to be a pastor. After finishing my four years of college and finding my wife, I set off for my four years of seminary training. At the young age of twenty-five, I was ordained into the Office of the Holy Ministry. After a short three-year stint at a church on the east end of Long Island where I interned and served my first call as an Associate Pastor, at twenty-seven years old, I was called to St. John's Lutheran Church, Sayville, to bring healing and hope to a badly divided and scarred community of faith.

Now, after eleven years of faithful service to those wonderful people, I as the shepherd, the healer, and the one called to bring hope found myself deeply in need of those things personally. I sat there in that large chair looking out at my flock feeling very small and broken. I sat there thinking to myself;

6

"How did I get in this place in my life?" But deep down I had a good idea of how I got there.

The last ten years of my personal life and my ministry (not to mention, my whole life) had been tumultuous in more ways than I care to remember. As my own family grew with each new child, I was more deeply engaged in contentious family battles with my dysfunctional, mentally ill, prescription drug-abusing, parents that required legal intervention. On the church front, I found myself ministering to families dealing with issues that literally made it to the front page of the newspaper. In the year leading up to Easter 2008, I presided over the funerals of four children of the church and community, all while going home and kissing my three young children ranging in age from nine to fifteen. In the midst of all of this, my marriage was falling apart, mostly of my own doing ….

How did I get here? Years of family trauma and dysfunction forced me to bottle up and beat down brokenness and insecurity. The pressures of ministry and the need to paint the perfect picture had me longing for a place to feel safe – to just be myself, warts and all. My wife and I got married before we both fully recognized the damage done by both our families of origin. This placed giant cement walls in front of true intimacy and honesty. Now, on the greatest and most important day in our faith as Christians, I felt impending death, not life.

Where was I on that Easter Sunday? I was a broken pastor who was wrestling with whether or not I should be serving in the church anymore. I was a broken father struggling as my oldest son was coming to terms with his homosexuality while serving in a church body that considered homosexuality a sin and unacceptable. I was a broken husband who no longer wanted to be married to my wife because I felt more alone when we were together than when I was alone. And, as if that was not enough, I had fallen in love with, and was involved with, a woman who was the step-mother of a Disney® star.

Yet though I was in the midst of a deep crisis right there in church on Easter, my personal journey through all of this would remind me of why the church is so necessary and important and why the church is a *sanctuary*.

<u>Sanctuary</u>

Noun

1 - a consecrated place such as the most sacred part of a religious building

-or-

the room in which general worship services are held

2 – a place of refuge and protection

3 – immunity from law attached to a sanctuary

Chapter 1
Epiphanies

It was the eighth-grade winter sports awards dinner at Long Island Lutheran Junior and Senior High School. LuHi, as it is affectionately referred to by all who have been part of it, and also how it is nationally known because of its basketball program, is a private Christian school on the north shore of Long Island. From the time of the writing of *The Great Gatsby*, this area of Long Island has been known as the *Gold Coast*. Multi-million-dollar mansions are the norm in this area. I rode the bus an hour each way and among these passengers, I was in the minority, as most of my schoolmates were of African American descent. As I rode the bus to come and go from LuHi, I would start my trip in Amityville riding past *the corner*, known for its drug dealing and impoverished homes, then pass the official Amityville Horror House, and finish by riding up winding Brookville Road, passing multiple mansions with three-, four-, and five- car garages to compliment their ten bedrooms and twelve bathrooms on their gated multi-acre horse properties. I remember the first time I went to a high school friend's party at one of these homes. I was fascinated and blown away by central vacuuming. I could not get over that you (or most likely the maid) just plugged the vacuum hose into the wall and the rug pollutants would just disappear.

My daily ride to this tuition-based private school would betray the reality of my family's life. We could not afford for me to attend LuHi. It was due to the generosity of my grandmother and a steep discount and scholarship from my home church, which was also Lutheran, that I was able to attend this school that would determine the direction of my life, right up to today. My childhood home was on the scale closer to the homes of North Amityville than to the mansions of Brookville.

I was thirteen years old on the night of the winter sports dinner and, for the first time in my life, I was allowed to participate in a team competitive sport – basketball. I made the team solely for the reason that I was the tallest person in the class, nearly six feet tall. My lack of real basketball ability was summed up in my whopping four total season points, all from free throws. These free throws were scored when I came off the bench for inconsequential moments in games where we were winning by an insurmountable lead. Our junior high school basketball team went undefeated that season and won the championship. My primary role on the team was as a cheerleader and benchwarmer, but that did not phase me or affect me. I was part of a team. I was involved in the comradery and the verbal jousting that marked and bonded together people who play on a team in organized sports. I felt like a normal person, doing normal things; and, for a brief period of time, some of the abnormality and chaos that marked my childhood home was hidden from me and the rest of the world.

As the team and I were sitting at our table finishing our dinner, I heard my teammates starting to laugh. They were pointing toward the entrance to the gym where family and friends, coming to celebrate the occasion, would enter. By this time in the evening, most of the guests had already arrived, but now at this moment, one latecomer entered into the building. My teammates and friends were pointing and laughing and I heard them say, "Look at the fat guy with the cane over there, with the hair sticking straight up on his head like a porcupine," and the laughter spread through the team table like the wave would take over a professional sporting event in the 1980s and 1990s. I looked up to where they were pointing and laughing, and, to my utter horror, I wanted to be sucked into and under my chair. In a pained and feeble voice, I said, "That's my father...." The laughter doubled in volume and intensity.

My father's appearance was, how shall I say it... rather unique. He was mostly bald, but he allowed the hair that he had to stick up straight on his head in the patchy areas where the hair would still grow. His hairstyle so traumatized me as I was growing up that for a long time my greatest fear in life was going bald. Ironically, this is something that I embrace now; and my children tell me repeatedly, as they look at old photos of me with hair, that I got much better looking without the hair. Anyway, my father had a rather large stomach that was highlighted by his choice of pants. He wore eyeglasses and shirts that came right out of the nerd guide for the 1970s.

The moment that he walked into the gym on that early spring evening stuck with me for years. I had long known that things were not exactly normal or right with my parents. Listening to the stories of friends around me regarding their parents' jobs, lives, and support of their activities always led me to feelings of jealousy and prayers that one day I would find adoption papers. But these thoughts were private – very few others knew what was going on inside me or our family home. That night at that table, the secret was out. I was not crazy, things were not right in my family, so much so that others like my teammates zeroed in on it in a matter of seconds.

The moment stirred up the first of many faith crises that I would wrestle with in my life. I knew, as a member of my family, along with all the teachings that I had heard in church, Sunday School, and at LuHi, that I should have been grateful, thankful, and proud that my father finally came to show some support for me and what I was doing. I had waited thirty-five regular season and playoff games for him to show up. But when he finally came, it was one of the most embarrassing moments in my short life. Because I could not embrace the moment for what it was intended to be, I was wracked with guilt and certainly felt less than the Christian that I thought God called me to be. This would not be the last time in my life that my faith calling battled with the reality of my life.

The word epiphany has become synonymous with Christian faith and practice. The event of the *Epiphany* twelve days after Christmas marks the visit of the Magi, the wise men, who followed the light of the star to visit the baby Jesus. The word *epiphany* comes from ancient Biblical Greek and means *light shining forth*. From those roots, one of the modern definitions for epiphany is *a sudden insight or intuitive understanding*.

Life is filled with epiphanies. Life in Christ is often a life filled with sudden insights and understandings – from celebrating the actual event of the Epiphany to all those moments where God's Spirit and presence shine light into the darkness of our lives, giving us insight and understanding. This book is a journey story. Like those Magi from afar, the story is filled with epiphanies. It is the story of my personal and professional journey through life and ministry highlighting the epiphanies that my Christian faith has granted to me through the blessing and gift of God's work in the Church. This is not a story of a "holier than thou" guy with a very pious and perfect family who works in a perfect church. No, this is a story about struggle and sin and imperfection and dysfunction and how the church, itself, not a perfect place filled with perfect people, has always been my safe place. The church has literally and figuratively been my *sanctuary*. Through this personal journey,

I have come to value and do everything in my power to make the church a sanctuary for those to whom I am called to minister.

The epiphany that I experienced in that LuHi gym over forty years ago would be the first of many regarding family systems, mental illness, and substance abuse. These insights that I have painfully gained throughout my life have helped me better understand and care for the people that God has entrusted to me throughout my work as a Lutheran pastor. Most importantly, these epiphanies have given me a deep appreciation and understanding of what it means when the Bible and the Church talk about, and live in, God's grace. The guilt that filled me for my reaction to my father's surprise appearance could only be overcome by receiving and understanding God's love and grace.

Nearly 1,500 years before the birth of Jesus, as Moses was called by God to lead the Israelites from their slavery at the hands of the Egyptians into the freedom of their new home in the promised land that would become known as Israel, God gave through Moses what has become known as the Ten Commandments. As Moses was leading the Israelites to become their own nation of people, he quickly became aware of the sin and brokenness that marks human life. This sin and imperfection find its roots in the first chapters of Genesis as we hear about the temptation in the Garden and the fall into sin. From that moment forward, human beings have been dealing with lives that have been less than perfect. Sin, sickness, incivility, jealousy, hatred, violence, and death are sad realities of human life. No matter how hard we try to overcome them, no matter how many laws are instituted to fight them, no matter how often we make excuses and wish things were not as they are, the harsh, cold fact and reality of human life is that sin and brokenness are inevitable, and the effects and consequences are passed down from generation to generation.

The explanation of the Ten Commandments, as Moses presented them to his newly formed nation and blended family, is the following: "I the LORD your God am a jealous God, punishing children for the iniquity of parents, to the third and the fourth generation of those who reject me, but showing steadfast love to the thousandth generation of those who love me and keep my commandments." (Exodus 20: 5b-6 NRSV). This simple and powerful explanation, offered up when God was giving His commandments to fight sin and evil, offers timeless insight and understanding to what is so often the case with the dysfunction that exists within families.

In family systems therapy, there is a concept that dysfunction is manifest over three to four generations and a multigenerational approach is needed for a family to overcome the issue that is plaguing and troubling the family. It never ceases to amaze me how the Bible, a book that is often seen and criticized by many as being an irrelevant, ancient book, is filled with so many timely truths and insights regarding human life and behavior. The point that God was making through Moses as He gave the Ten Commandments is that sin and dysfunction manifests themselves in ways that are passed on from parents to children and, if not addressed, to grandchildren and great-grandchildren.

We see evidence of this cycle of sin and dysfunction every time we go to a doctor for the first time. Before we enter the doctor's examining room, we fill out lengthy questionnaires that ask for all the family history regarding every known disease and unpronounceable word that relates to our bodies and health. If we go to a qualified mental health professional, that person will dig deep into our past experiences, especially in regard to our families of origin because there is often a direct link between our current mental health and struggles and the history that has led us to that moment of crisis. In politics and government, it is often said that history repeats itself. This phrase is used as an encouragement for our leaders to learn and understand the things that have happened in the past because those same thoughts, agendas, and philosophies, are being repeated today.

In families, there is the generation where the problem or dysfunction reveals itself for the first time. The children of that generation are directly impacted by the issues, often in ways that are not realized and understood until later in life. Then that generation, hopefully, becomes aware of the problem in a way that gives them the courage to begin a process of addressing the dysfunction so that healing and rebuilding can take place. If this does not start with this generation, the problem or dysfunction will continue to manifest itself in the next generation, the grandchildren, and so on, until somewhere along the way, the family is acted on by an outside force that can begin to address the issue. For the cycle of sin and dysfunction to be interrupted in a way that leads to health and healing, an epiphany needs to take place. These unhealthy, painful, and broken deeds, often hidden in the darkness, need to have light shined on them.

Throughout my life, as I hope you will come to see, it has been the Church, built upon the grace and love of Jesus Christ, that has been that outside force and safe place where light has shined on and through the darkness. It's important to note and remember that when God spoke those words of explanation to Moses as He gave the Ten Commandments, that, though the effects of sin with its consequences affect the third and fourth generation, God goes on to say that His love goes on for thousands of generations. That is how God, in the Bible, does math. Sadly, the Bible and the Judeo-Christian faith are often perceived as a religion that takes pleasure in punishment and the chastisement of people, especially when they mess up or fail. Nothing could be further from the true heart and message of the Bible. God acknowledges the reality of the sin and brokenness that tears apart lives and destroys our world. From that acknowledgment, the story that is the theme and thread that ties together the entirety of the Sacred Scriptures, written over thousands of years, is that God is moved to help, heal, and free us from the pain and death brought by sin and dysfunction. In the early words of the Bible, as we hear about Adam and Eve's disobedience and the consequences of it, we immediately hear God offer the hope of healing that will come through the offspring of Eve, who will come to crush the head of the serpent (Genesis 3:15). This promise will become the thread the winds its way through Scripture leading us to Jesus. That thread is our hope. Though all people sin and are broken, it is according to God's unique method of doing math that the love and sacrifice of the One, Jesus Christ, releases the infinite numbers of broken sinners.

It's all about epiphanies. God wants the light of hope and healing to break forth into our lives, sheltering us in God's loving presence and through the community that is the Church, to bring to us healing and new life.

Chapter 2
A Long Time Ago...

Star Wars had (and still has) a profound impact upon my life as it did on just about every other child born sometime in the 1970s. Next to God, *Star Wars* is right up there. This will not be the last time that you encounter a *Star Wars* story or reference. In April 1981, the first *Star Wars* movie, simply known then as *Star Wars* had its title expanded to *Star Wars: Episode IV – A New Hope*. When this change was made to the re-release of the movie and the famous opening scroll, which set the background of the story, I remember being filled with great excitement because the rumored news (long before the internet and spoilers) was that we were going to get a lot more of the story. In fact, the reason *Star Wars* was numbered "Episode IV" was because we were going to get the origin story behind Darth Vader and many of the other beloved characters (all of which I owned as action figures, and still do to this day). It would take another sixteen years after *Return of the Jedi* was released for us to begin to get the origin story, but it did eventually come when *The Phantom Menace* was released in 1999.

Origin stories are an important part of our life's journey and identity. Over the past few decades, the entertainment industry has fully embraced the art of origin storytelling. We have seen movies, read books, and watched TV shows that have gone back in time to help the audience better understand the circumstances and events that led to the beloved characters that we have embraced. From the *Star Wars* prequel trilogy to

Batman Begins to *Wicked* to the reimagined cast of the original *Star Trek*, Hollywood has come to see the value and need for the public's consumption of what came before we were introduced to the story.

By knowing the story behind the story, we come to better understand what motivates and drives the person, character, or institution that interests or impacts us in life. Origin stories help with identity, and identity is an essential part of life. Marketing, branding, and logos are all about telling an origin story that better focuses the purpose, mission, and identity of that person, product, or institution being marketed. In families, whether it be our biological families or our spiritual families, the origin story is essential to where we are in our life's journey today.

My origin story began in January 1970. My mother told me I was supposed to be a sixties child, but I came three weeks after her due date. I like this because I do not have to think too hard about how old I am. Because I was born in early January 1970, my age in years will always match the fourth digit of the year. I just need to remember the decade. So, in 2023, I turned fifty-three years old. I didn't like being born in January because I was always the youngest person in the class. Although, when everyone was turning fifty, and I was still in my forties, that was pretty cool.

My childhood home was a two-story cinder block, flat-roof house with no front door. It was the weirdest house in the neighborhood. The windows were very small, except for the one big bay window that faced the backyard. You had to walk up a side path to the main door on the left side of the house. As you looked at the house from the street, you couldn't find the front door. The house was situated on a canal that fed from the Great South Bay on Long Island's south shore. We had a small brick-paved backyard. I hated the yard. There was no grass that we could play on. I had to constantly pull the weeds in between the bricks, and it was never even because the sand underneath the backyard was slowly sinking into the canal. For many years early in my life, there was a decaying seventeen-foot wooden Criss Craft cabin cruiser that sat in the water, all year round. We never ever took the boat out for a cruise. It just sat there, peeling and rotting. My father kept saying that he was going to fix it up so we could use it, but it never happened. This would become a common theme in my life with my parents.

Until I was around 7 years old, life in my family home appeared to be relatively normal. My father went to work at the telephone company. My mother stayed at home and cared for me and my sister, who was four years younger than me. My mother would bake and sew and help out with school events and trips.

My parents both played the organ, and that is how they met. I grew up with two organs in the living room of our home, but I never learned how to play them. My mother would try to give me lessons, but it is a challenge for parents to teach their own children. My mother told me that one day I would regret not learning, and she was right. One of the biggest regrets that I have in my life is that I never learned how to play the organ or the piano. As a pastor in a church tradition that loves to sing and has a deep personal appreciation for the gift of music, I wish I had heeded my mother's advice.

When I was seven years old, there was a bad hurricane that blew through Long Island. My father was called into work that night at the phone company. The story goes that, at some time during his shift, he had to climb a ladder up to the roof of the telephone building to fix a generator that powered the phones. On his way back down the ladder, he somehow slipped. He did not fall all the way to the ground but caught himself again on the ladder. Supposedly, the sharp jerking and trauma of grabbing the ladder as he was falling caused a back injury that stayed with him the rest of his life. From that day forward, as a seven-year-old, I never saw my father regularly go to work again.

In the years that followed, my father's medical condition spiraled negatively. The year after the ladder accident, he had an apparent heart attack. By my teenage years, my father spent the majority of the day in bed. He would not get up until after twelve noon. He would head back to bed at intermittent times during the day.

As a result of this, my mother was forced to go back to work full-time. She held down a position for a few years as an administrative assistant in a telecommunications company. For a few years, she was the breadwinner and the more functional, visible parent in the family. Unfortunately, when I was eleven years old, that too would change. My mother was involved in a car accident that laid her up for weeks. Not long after the car accident, she started to experience numbness on one side of her body along with minor seizures. After several years of consulting medical professionals, she was diagnosed with multiple sclerosis. Just like that, by the time I was a teenager, both my parents were at home full-time on disability.

During my high school years, the story of my family seemed to be pretty straightforward. My parents were unlucky people who, through a series of unfortunate events, were dealt a short hand in life. But as I moved on to college and adulthood, and as I came to better understand our entire family and origin story, the circumstances surrounding my parents and their misfortune were not so clear and easy to pinpoint.

For as long as I can remember, prescription medications were strewn all over our home. In the hallway leading to my parents' bedroom was a closet that people would normally fill with clothes or towels or cleaning instruments. This closet was packed full from top to bottom, with shelves on the door that opened, with medical equipment and prescription drugs. The nightstands, on either side of my parents' bed, were covered with pill containers. The top of the refrigerator in the kitchen regularly had big vials of Codeine®, Darvon®, Valium®, Percocet®, and other narcotic prescription drugs.

When I obtained my driver's license at seventeen, one of the first places I drove to was the pharmacy in Amityville. I would take a triplicate written prescription for special narcotic drugs to the pharmacist's window and then drive home with these drugs. If I had not been such a good, clueless, "holy" kid, I could have made a fortune on the street corner in Amityville. What I figured out later on in life is that, while I was driving the prescriptions to the corner drug store, my parents were also sending away for three-month supplies from the mail-in pharmacy. This was the 1980s before everything was computerized like it is today. In hindsight, this was a big problem in the eighties. People would have multiple doctors, who wouldn't know what the other doctors were prescribing, and patients would play the system for legalized drug addiction.

After my mother's accident, each parent fed off of the other's addiction and delusional thinking, justifying their behavior because they "needed the medicines for pain." This dysfunctional cycle sadly continued throughout the rest of their lives.

The consequences of this lifestyle on me and my sister are our origin story. The need for us to be the caretakers for our parents, and the circumstances that surrounded this, placed both of us on vocational paths that led us to help others–me as a pastor, my sister as a physician's assistant. Often, those who needed help themselves go into helping professions.

By the time we were teenagers, we were the homemakers. We were responsible for the household chores.

When the house was cleaned, we were the ones who did it. But this was a monumental task. Along with the drug addiction and mental illness came delusional thinking about what our parents needed and could do, leading to hoarding. The decaying boat in the backyard was just the beginning. We lived on the second story of our home. The first story was filled with unfinished projects, a very expensive wood shop that never got used, and loads of half-repaired computers, along with every published computer magazine from the 1980s. None of this stuff was organized. It was strewn all over the place wherever it fell. There was rarely a path where the real floor could be seen on that first floor. Over time, as the dysfunction and drug addiction aggregated, the mess and the hoarding made its way to the second floor where we lived. There were computers on the dining room table and unplayed music on the organs. My parents' bedroom was a cauldron of chaos and disorganization. There was hardly a path to walk around my parents' bed. My mother's side of the bed was crowded with piles of clothes needing to be sewn or cleaned or given away (which never happened). My father's side of the bed was an avalanche of fallen magazine piles that, someday my dad was going to read. There was a television on the dresser at the foot of the bed that became the balancing point for a bunch of other items that would never see a use in life. Natural light from the bedroom windows was never allowed to enter their room. To this day, I have to open the blinds in all the rooms I am in as soon as I get up, and I cannot tolerate a cabinet door that is left open. When there is so much disarray and chaos, I clamored for control, cleanliness, and order.

I am an expert Tetris®-like packer when it comes to grocery bags and the trunk of the car because of this time in my parents' life. From about the age of eleven on, I would do the majority of the food shopping. Most of the time I had to ride my bike to the food store. I had this ugly yellow bike that the neighborhood kids would make fun of because it had a big basket on the front. The basket was wide enough to hold two brown grocery bags. My mother would give me a list and money and I would ride my bike to Key Food®, about a mile from the house. I would go shopping and get what we needed on the list. I would pack my own grocery bags because I knew that I had to get everything perfectly balanced into those two brown bags so that I could pedal home without the bike steering too much to one side. Thank God those brown paper bags were not outlawed until after I went to college. I can't imagine what I would have done riding home on that bike with plastic bags – two on the handlebars, three tied to my seat, two between my legs ... but I digress.

After I went to college, my sister, sadly, had to deal with the brunt of this dysfunction. With me no longer at home to carry some of the load, it all fell on her. In addition to our parents' deepening drug addiction, their already unstable financial situation continued to deteriorate; and they mentally tortured her by threatening to move from New York to Pennsylvania before she graduated from high school. At one point my sister's friends had a going away party for her; but then, like so many other times before, my parents did not follow through.

While I was at college and my sister was at home, my parents decided that they were going to purchase an old commuter bus from Minnesota for $5000 and convert it into their dream recreational home. You can begin to fathom the depth of their delusional thinking with this purchase. Two people who didn't get out of bed before noon, who hadn't used a power tool in years, who lived in a house itself that needed fixing up, were going to renovate a forty-foot diesel bus!

The older my sister and I got, the more we were able to

remove ourselves from our childhood home, and the more we were allowed to connect with other relatives. From this, we could more clearly see the dysfunction for what it was. More questions were raised regarding the circumstances that started this whole cycle of brokenness.

When we were younger children, as our parents slowly disintegrated into their addiction and dysfunction, they would remove themselves from normal interactions with family, friends, and the general public. I believe that deep down my parents knew that things were not right or normal, and dysfunction doesn't want to be exposed. Before I was a teenager, I remember going to family gatherings, especially at the holidays, and loving being with family. By the time I was a teenager, rarely if ever did we gather with relatives. The most important relative that we were not allowed to see too often was my father's sister, Aunt Carolee, and her husband, Uncle Bill. As my life moved forward toward maturity and eventual healing, Aunt Carolee and Uncle Bill would become the most important extended family that I would have in my life.

Aunt Carolee battled and triumphed over her own family dysfunction. She tells stories that have helped to focus more clearly some of the issues with my father. From a young age, my aunt recalls that my father was an angry, nasty, and abusive child. This was not helped by her mother (my grandmother) who would co-dependently enable my father's behavior right up to the day she died. When my father was facing the Vietnam draft, my grandmother wrote countless letters, all the way up to her senator, to keep my father out of the draft because he had flat feet and a bad back. This was one of the many examples of how my grandmother would coddle, protect, and excuse away my father's behavior. My grandmother's sheltering and protection of my father (while completely ignoring my aunt) would lead my father to be a weak person who could not stand up to adversity or a challenge. In the later years of her life, my grandmother admitted that if mental health therapy had been a thing when my father was a child, she would have gotten him help.

Due to this unhealthy family environment that my aunt grew up in (that third and fourth generation stuff), my aunt married an emotionally unavailable alcoholic man who often was absent from the marriage and family. After her divorce, my aunt, while raising her two children, went on to gain degrees in psychology, social work, and family systems therapy. Many of the insights and epiphanies that I have gained regarding my family and are alluded to on these pages are thanks in part to Aunt Carolee and Uncle Bill, her second husband.

But it took a long time to get there. Because we were not allowed to get together with family relatives because of my parents' fear of the dysfunction being exposed, I wasn't socially acclimated enough to be comfortable with my aunt and uncle. When Aunt Carolee married Uncle Bill, we would only see them once or twice a year. Uncle Bill, having wrestled and overcome his own family demons, was a rather direct and opinionated yet extremely funny guy. For a long time, I was terrified of Uncle Bill. He always had something to say, and it always made sense, and was very intelligent. If he didn't like something, you knew it. So, on the few occasions we were able to see family, I kept my distance.

That all changed on the first weekend in August 1983 when I was thirteen years old. I remember the date because it was the first week that Z100 started with pop music on New York radio. My aunt and uncle had recently purchased a house in Montauk, the farthest east you can go on Long Island before you swim to England. Montauk is another seaside fishing community on the south fork of Long Island that played host to the homes of EB White, the author of *Charlotte's Webb*, Paul

Simon, and my favorite musician, Billy Joel.

To celebrate the new house, Aunt Carolee and Uncle Bill had a summer party. My mother was feeling well enough to attend so we drove the two hours to Montauk. Of course, my father was too sick to go. We listened to Z100 on the car radio all the way out on the ride. I remember the joy of this day– seeing family and relatives again and being "normal." The greatest part of the day was when Uncle Bill, knowing I was a baseball fan, took me down to the beach to throw the baseball with me. I know that this was not a big deal for my uncle, but it meant the world to me and opened the door to a relationship that would profoundly change my life. One of my greatest desires throughout my childhood was to play catch with my father, to do the normal things that you imagine that a father and a son would do together. (This will play itself out in a different way with my first son). I am a huge baseball fan. I remember when my mother took me to my first Yankees game. Every day during the summer, I would play wiffle ball with some friends in the neighborhood. But I never got to play with my father. When Uncle Bill took me alone to the beach and spent that time playing catch with me, even though I was a terrible baseball player, it made me feel loved. It made me feel valued. It made me feel normal. This would be the first step in many steps with my aunt and uncle leading to a beginning sense of normalcy.

Through the years, this relationship with Aunt Carolee and Uncle Bill would provide information on and insight into our entire family. While they were aware that there were things about my home life that were not right, they could never get close enough to truly see and understand what was going on. Together, as we built a relationship, we all were able to piece together facts and events to get a better sense and picture of what was going on. Through this relationship and all that we struggled with and shared, unhealthy behaviors and thoughts began to be replaced with healthier ones. Aunt Carolee and Uncle Bill were the first of many gifts that God would bring into my life to put His hand around me and lead me to where I needed to go.

From all the information that we have discovered about my parents and the rest of the family, I have come to reconsider the unfortunate circumstances that befell my parents. I've come to a sense of peace wondering in a certain sense which came first. Because I was so young at the time, I cannot be sure if my father's accident led to his substance abuse or if substance abuse led to the accident. The same holds true for my mother's car accident. In the end, it doesn't really matter. Ultimately, the entire situation, no matter what the cause, is the result of sin. Sin is that imperfection and brokenness that plagues the world. Sin needs the remedy that comes from the sanctuary of God's grace.

Chapter 3
The Need for Sanctuary

My tenth birthday in January 1980 should have been a big, exciting day. I was turning double digits–a decade old. I felt so grown up. An event like this, adding another digit column to my life, would not happen again for ninety years! But the day itself, as a birthday, kinda sucked. The reason is that on that day my other grandparents, on my mother's side, moved into a house two houses from my family home. All day I waited for birthday cake and my presents, but everyone was busy with the move. We finally celebrated my birthday after eight o'clock right before I went to bed.

When all is said and done, my tenth birthday was not the real problem or issue with the serious boundary and privacy violation that was the move of my mother's parents. No, there were much deeper and darker problems hiding from the light.

These grandparents were not, in fact, my mother's biological parents. The woman I knew as "grandma" was actually the sister of my mother's biological mother. According to rumors that were rarely ever spoken in the 1970s, my mother's biological mother was a promiscuous woman who was not sure who my mother's father was. In the midst of her instability, she recognized that she could not care for my mother; therefore her sister, who already had five of her own natural children; took custody of my mother. My mother became the sixth, and I believe the youngest member of that family.

For as long as I can remember, my grandmother was a bedridden stroke victim. She could not use the left side of her body, and she could not speak very well. Before my tenth birthday, they lived in Bellmore, a town about a half hour from my parents. After the neighbors who lived in the house two houses from mine died, my parents thought it would be a great idea if my grandparents moved two houses from us so that–get this–my parents could help take care of them. There's that delusional thinking again.

My grandfather on my mother's side was a retired city bus mechanic. From the time of my grandmother's stroke, he diligently cared for my grandmother–caring for her skin so that she didn't get bedsores, turning her from side to side, and cooking, cleaning, and transferring her to the bedpan when needed.

Even though my grandmother was bedridden and was hard to communicate with, she still found ways to love me in the best way that she could. Every time I came over to see her and gave her a kiss, she would open the drawer of her nightstand with her good arm and give me a dollar. She introduced me to her favorite television program–professional wrestling! From the first time I saw it, I fell in love with the art and craft of "wrasslin'." She also, and I still to this day cannot believe I am writing this, introduced me to the Playboy channel. When this channel first came to cable TV in late 1980, I would occasionally come over to my grandparents' and walk into my grandmother's bedroom and she would be watching softcore porn on the TV. She wouldn't change it when I came in. But when my grandfather or my mother came by, she would quickly flip the channel. This would be just the beginning of the boundary issues at my grandparents' house.

Unlike my parents, my grandfather was a very organized and handy fellow. He wouldn't hesitate to fix something that was broken. When he saw me and my friends playing wiffle ball and watched us throwing pitches against the garage door, he made a nice backdrop with a delineated strike zone. The tools that he used to make this were all hung perfectly on the back wall of the garage. He outlined each tool and painted the shape of each tool, so he knew exactly where to return the tool when he finished with it. One day I dropped one of his hammers into the canal, and it could not be recovered. From that day forward, every time I went into the garage, I had to look at the black outline of a missing hammer with the handwritten note "dropped in the canal by Harry" with the date under it.

From the time after my tenth birthday, my sister and I would, on almost a daily basis for one reason or another, go over to my grandparents' house. Sometimes, it was because my parents were sleeping. Sometimes, it was just to have fun in their backyard–they had grass! And a pool! And, I could fish off their dock without the danger of the yard caving in and taking me with it. Sometimes, I went over so I could do some shopping for my grandfather, just like I did for my parents. On more than one occasion, my grandfather would send me to the store with a twenty-dollar bill to come home with a carton of Camel cigarettes. I am still not sure how I was allowed to buy the cigarettes. But it happened often. It would be this exposure to my grandfather's smoking habit that would keep me from ever smoking. After he died, and my father miraculously found some energy to get the house ready to sell because he and my mom would get the money, we went through gallons of Fantastic® brand cleaning spray to clean the walls of the house. As soon as we soak-sprayed the walls, the fluid would roll down the walls a deep dark black color. For months, the smell of that fluid would linger in my nose. Anytime I see someone smoking today, I am immediately mentally transported back to that summer cleaning my grandfather's house, picturing what the inside of a smoker's lungs look like.

The first time in my life that I learned that a pastor did more than just wear some interesting clothes and speak some godly words on a Sunday was the day that my parents found out that my grandfather was rumored to be sexually abusing family members. Though I do not remember the date of this discovery, I remember the scene as if it were yesterday and not forty years ago.

There were many tears and shouts of anger. The house was in complete chaos and unrest. My home church pastor knocked on the door and came into the home. We sat down together as a family and the pastor led the discussion. He asked us questions about the situation. The pastor brought a calm to the situation with the assurance that God was still present. He prayed with us and assured us that he would be there for us. And, as we moved forward from that day, he *was* there for us, in the most challenging of situations.

Sadly, and unfortunately, sexual abuse among families is all too common. In those days, these family secrets were often taken to the grave by many families, further impacting the emotional, spiritual, and sexual damage to those who were victims of the abuse. Families are as sick as their secrets! My family is no exception to this reality. Our family's pain and dysfunction, was further exacerbated by how my parents chose to handle the aftermath of the situation.

In my years of service as a pastor, I have come to believe and observe that sexual sins are the worst and most devastating sins that can ever be committed toward another person. Murder is up there on the list of sins, but the victim's pain ends at the moment of death. Sexual sins gut the identity, the confidence, the trust, and the emotional health of the person who has been victimized and usually remain with that person for the rest of their earthly lives. My heart breaks every time I am called to minister to an individual who has been sexually abused by someone else. I am also sickened that the recent history of the Christian church has been marked by this sin and the failure to deal with it justly.

The sinister part of all this lies in what transpired by the time both my grandparents died. My grandmother died in 1986 and my grandfather died in 1989. By the time they both were dead, my parents had managed to bleed my grandparents for every dollar they had. After their deaths, my parents inherited the house. Somehow, my mother's five natural brothers and sister were written out of the will. I never saw them again after the funeral. I can only conclude that, because my parents were sick on so many levels, and because they were financially strapped because of their sickness, they used this alleged sexual abuse situation to blackmail, manipulate, and leverage my grandfather into buying them off at a price.

The timing of this traumatic family event correlates very closely with the intensifying of my parent's decay physically and mentally. I don't know if it was a coincidence or as a result of the damage done by this horrific sin. Either way, again, it doesn't matter. That's sin and the brokenness it brings.

Yet, in the midst of this trauma and terror, the hand of God was at work, as it always is at work. Romans 8:28 (NRSV) reminds us that, "We know that all things work together for good for those who love God, who are called according to his purpose." The promise of God's love and grace is that God does not abandon us, especially at those times when sin and evil are working the hardest.

The pastor's presence amid this horror was not a one-off

event. From that day forward, even though my parents' attendance and participation at the church was minimal at best, the pastor, the youth director, and our friends from the church were a constant, affirming, loving presence in our lives.

When they were awake enough for him to visit, my pastor would come to visit my parents at home and would bring them communion. When we couldn't make it to church, they arranged for us to receive a special phone call on Sunday mornings at eleven a.m. whereby we could place the phone into a special speaker unit and listen to the Sunday Service. I did many a sermon report for confirmation class sitting next to the telephone. Over time, as it became more clear that my parents would never feel good enough to get up for church, the youth director or some other adult would pick me up and take me to church.

After I was confirmed in eighth grade, I was asked to teach Sunday School to kindergarten children. Even though I had no business doing this, I was welcomed openly, and I continued to do this for many years.

In every way possible, the church–by church, I mean all the people who make up the church like the pastor, the youth leader, the Sunday school teachers, other adults, and my teenage friends–all went out of their way to be there for my family. In the aftermath of this terrible family revelation, and in the ongoing midst of the dysfunction that was my parents' drug addiction, sickness, and mental illness, I slowly began to see and know that the church was a sanctuary.

From this terrible event that marked my family's history, God slowly began to set me on the journey that would lead me into the Holy Ministry with my calling to make sure that the church is a sanctuary for others.

Chapter 4
O Come, O Come, Emmanuel

The altar looked completely different from any other time I had been in church. Beautiful white linens adorned the altar where the stainless-steel vessels for the holy communion sat, while several red and white poinsettia plants started at the top of the altar and were placed all the way down to the floor and all the way along the floor down the aisle lining each side of the choir pews. To the left of the altar was an eight-foot tree with red lights and red apples, representing the tree of the knowledge of good and evil that led to the forbidden fruit of temptation in the Garden of Eden. To the right of the altar stood another eight-foot tree. This one had white lights and was decorated with beautiful white and gold Chrismon ornaments. Chrismons are handmade decorations in the church that are in the shape of crosses, mangers, sheep, anchors, stars, seashells, and many other Biblical symbols that remind us of the story of salvation. Evergreen roping outlined the main archway leading up to the altar of the church while other sets of evergreen roping were hung intermittently from the crossbeams and balcony of the church. At the end of each pew, hung candelabras with candles burning.

It was the late service on Christmas Eve 1981 at St. Paul's Lutheran Church in Amityville, New York. This was the first time a Christmas Eve Service in Church really impacted me and stood out for me. I remember sitting on the right side of the church, just in front of the pulpit where the pastor would deliver his Christmas message. My mother and I were about five pews back from the front of the church. It was just my mother and me in church, because again, my father was not feeling well enough to join us, so my sister went to bed early because she stayed home with him.

Between the first and second reading, one of the members of the church choir stood up in the choir loft and made her way to the front of the church. As she stood there in the center of the aisle, she pulled out her violin, and began to play "O Holy Night." I had never heard the hymn before. At eleven years old, I was raptured by it and captivated by the intent and the emotion that she put into her effort of playing the hymn for the crowded church. When she completed the song, I looked over at my mother and my mother had tears flowing down her face. Though I would not fully understand this until later on in my life, I instinctively knew that this was a special moment and that the church was a special place.

In spite of the sin and dysfunction that marred our family, my parents did love my sister and me and did the best that they could with what they had in life. Our life was marked by chaos and sickness, yet there were those times when my parents would rise out of the darkness to show us love. Christmas was always one of those times, so much so that my parents went way overboard with the gifts that we received at Christmas. It was a sinful example of greed and gluttony–but we sure did benefit from it! Almost every Christmas, we received most of the gifts that we asked for on our Christmas list. The entire couch next to the Christmas tree would be piled with beautifully wrapped boxes of Christmas presents. I have often wondered if the loot of treasures we opened on Christmas morning was their way of assuaging the guilt they felt for the way we were living.

But aside from the gifts, one of the biggest and best

things that I could count on every Christmas is that the house would be cleaner, better smelling, and cozier to live in at Christmastime. Now, of course, my sister and I had to do most of the cleaning and the decorating, but it was the one time of year that we didn't mind because we knew what was coming after the house was decorated.

The clutter and messiness of our house was just about everywhere we turned. We had a small deck on the second level outside of the house. It was some ten feet up in the air. The entire space below the deck was piled with old fencing, empty 55-gallon drums, and other outdoor junk that should have been taken away by a scrap metal dealer years earlier. The aluminum outdoor shed we had on the other side of the house was nearly impossible to open because lawn tools, hoses, and outdoor toys were haphazardly tossed inside with no order; the doors had to be quickly slammed shut so nothing fell out. Like the shed, the entire first floor of the house was a hoarder's dream filled with unfinished projects as well as tools and equipment that would never be used to their full potential.

Those projects and tools were a sad testimony to my father's unrealized potential. My father was a very smart man. He bordered on having a photographic memory. He could read up on how to build or fix something one time and when he set his mind to it and had the energy, he could do it on the first try. The first color television that we had in our home was a Heathkit® TV. From 1947 until 1992, Heathkit® produced building kits for televisions, radios, and other electronics that smart, engineering-type people could put together themselves. Anytime that TV my father built had a problem, he was able to take it apart and fix it again. I also remember a time when I was an early teenager when I helped my father, who must have been feeling a little better, cut through the first and second floor of our home and install a circular stairway, so that we no longer needed to go outside to enter the first floor of the house. This was no simple accomplishment that just anyone off the street would be able to achieve without caving the second floor into the first floor. Yet even though he installed this staircase, he never fully completed it. He never installed the wood oak treads for each step. For years, I found myself moving the pile of wood treads from place to place amid the mess of the house. My father had potential and ability, but he sadly never lived up to the God-given talent that was bestowed upon him. The evidence of this cluttered our house year after year after year.

But Christmas broke through all of this. When the house was decorated for Christmas and the tree was lit all day and cinnamon candles were lit at night and Christmas carols were playing on the stereo system, for a short time there was peace in our home and joy in our world. To this day, Christmas is my favorite time of year, thanks in part to this peaceful and calm sentiment that broke into the dysfunctional atmosphere of our lives. Every year I look forward to decorating my house and the church for Christmas. I can't wait for Santa to arrive at the end of the Macy's Thanksgiving Day parade, ushering in the official start of the holiday season. Of the few items that I still have from my childhood home, the ones that I wanted the most, are the Nikko® Christmas Dinner plates and other items that we gifted to my mother every year for Christmas and her birthday, which was on New Year's Day.

Before I ever thought about becoming a pastor, this annual visit of Christmas joy and peace each year at home and in the church, served as a living object lesson of what the real message and gift of Christmas are all about. At the heart of the Christmas message in the Bible is the presence of God and God's love breaking into the sin, chaos, and dysfunction of the world.

At the heart of the Biblical Christmas message is the

word "incarnation." This is the fancy theological word that points to how God became human and came into the world. Up until Jesus, every god who was worshipped and called upon by humanity was far off. They were gods set way up in the sky, or heaven, or wherever, and humans had to petition, please, and do good, to earn the favor and blessing of the god. There was nothing personal or intimate about these gods.

With the entering of Jesus into the world through the womb of His mother Mary, God became incarnate. God put on human flesh and came near. This concept of God being in the flesh and near is at the heart of what sets apart the comfort and the hope that we have. In Jesus, we have the assurance that God does understand what we go through and deal with as human beings. I often shock and joke around with my confirmation students (middle school-age children) by saying, "Do you ever think about Jesus dropping a deuce?!" For those unfamiliar with that phrase, it is doing "number two" in the bathroom. Of course, the response is "No way" or "Ewww." Yet, as irreverent as this image is for our Savior, it makes a very important point about why Jesus is so precious to us and brings us so much comfort and hope. For yes, Jesus did have to excuse Himself, probably each day like the rest of us, and go to the bathroom. Jesus experienced puberty. Jesus experienced sweat and exhaustion. From these little things that we can relate to when God became human comes the comfort of knowing that Jesus also experienced, knew, and dealt with the emotions that the sin, pain, and brokenness of this world brings to people. The message of Christmas is that Jesus gets us and understands us, and that motivates Jesus to save us.

When Matthew's Gospel tells the story of the angel's appearing to Joseph foretelling the birth of Jesus, we hear the following:

"Joseph, son of David, do not be afraid to take

Mary as your wife, for the child conceived in her is from the Holy Spirit. She will bear a son, and you are to name him Jesus, for he will save his people from their sins." All this took place to fulfill what had been spoken by the Lord through the prophet: "Look, the virgin shall conceive and bear a son, and they shall name him Emmanuel," which means, "God is with us." (Matthew 1: 20a-23 NRSV)

One of the most important and beautiful parts of God's plan for our lives is that our faith assures us that we are not alone and that there is hope–no matter what we are experiencing in life. Whether we celebrate the secular or the religious aspects of Christmas, they both serve as reminders of the same thing. I have noticed that over the past few years, especially in the midst of the pandemic, people have been decorating their homes for Christmas earlier and earlier. Throughout my life, it seemed to me that there was an unwritten rule that you never decorated for Christmas before Thanksgiving. Only malls and department stores did such a thing! But as the darkness and doom of the last few years has hung over us and the entire world, I have found that people were looking for the light and the hope that is often exemplified in the decorations of Christmas. So that unwritten rule has been freely broken by many in the hopes of having a little joy and peace. That's the power and message of Christ and Christmas.

When Christmas came each year and broke into the darkness of my family's home, it was beginning to set the stage for me to truly and deeply understand how that message of Christmas breaks into all the world and how God would use me to help spread that message.

As I moved into high school, Christmas at the church would continue to grow in importance as part of my celebration of the holiday. Not only would I come to better know and understand the traditional Biblical Christmas story, but I would also be used by my pastor more intentionally in the work of the church. It would start in early December when I would be asked to help some of the men at the church set up the huge outdoor nativity set. We had to drag this enclosed house on a trailer into the front yard of the church. We had to clean all the cobwebs and other dirt that accumulated since last Christmas and then we had to put back in place all of the nativity figures with a new batch of hay while making sure that the lighting was just right. By tenth grade, my pastor asked me to assist him every year at the three Christmas Eve Services. This meant that I would put on one of the white robes worn by the assistants. I would sit in front across from the pastor. Many a Christmas Eve my pastor would look across at me and make a motion for me to squeeze my legs together because I was slouching and *man-spreading* before it was officially a thing. I would read the Old Testament and Epistle lessons. I would lead the congregation into the Creed. Then I would assist in distributing the Sacrament of the Altar. As a teenager, I didn't realize what a privilege that was. For the most part, I was excited to be there because, every Christmas Eve, in between the two late services, there would be a giant six-foot hero sandwich in the church kitchen that the choir and everyone who helped on Christmas Eve would get to eat together. As a growing teenage boy, this was one of my favorite Christmas Eve activities at church.

Today, as a pastor who has served in the church for thirty years, I have come to appreciate the enormous privilege and responsibility that I have every Christmas. I know that on Christmas (and then again on Easter) there are many people who are coming to the church who may never have been there before or may not have been there in a while. From my own experience, I want them to have Christmas (and Christ) break through whatever darkness they may be surrounded by. Thoughts and themes for my Christmas message start in the fall and come to a crescendo on Christmas Eve. At the heart of that message, each year is making it very clear that God is with us.

When pastors have the privilege of serving in a church for a longer period of time, we get to know the lives and families of the people to whom we are called to serve. At Christmas, and every time I serve in church, as people come forward to the altar to receive Holy Communion, I think of the struggles that I know those people are carrying. As I place in their hands the bread, and as they receive the cup of wine, I am personally carrying to them the message of Christmas. The Church's teaching regarding the Holy Communion, also known as the *Lord's Supper* and the *Holy Eucharist*, and the *Sacrament of the Altar* is that, in a miraculous way that will never make sense to us rationally or intellectually, the body and blood of Jesus are carried with the bread and wine to the person to whom it is being given. It is literally "God is with us." As God came into the world through the womb of Mary on that Christmas night so long ago, God keeps coming to us in the church, especially through the Sacrament of Holy Communion.

When God comes to us in the midst of whatever dysfunction, chaos, and brokenness that exists in our lives, we find safety, we find hope, we find love, and we find sanctuary.

Chapter 5
The Call and Hand of God

It was May 1987, a few weeks before I would graduate from LuHi. The entire school gathered for one of the last weekly chapel services of the year. Our chapel services were not held in a chapel-like building. Each week we would all gather in the gym that was large enough to hold three full basketball courts. The hard, wooden bleachers on one side of the gym would all be fully pulled out and the entire school population from seventh to twelfth grade, about four hundred fifty students, would sit on these bleachers for Scripture, song, and inspiration. The remaining two basketball courts would be darkened, and all the light would shine on those leading chapel nearest to us in front of the bleachers. This would be an important reminder that God can work anywhere in anyone, not just in a fancy, prescribed church building.

Throughout my years at LuHi, chapel was organized and led by Pastor Ron. He, along with my pastor from my home church in Amityville, would be one of the main influences in God's leading me to become a pastor. Pastor Ron was a single guy. He was somewhat flighty, like the absent-minded professor. You could never be fully sure that Pastor Ron was going to show up to an appointment. But his flightiness is what made him so easily relatable to teenagers. He could fully relate to us when we forgot our homework or lunch or whatever it might have been, which made it much easier for all of us to talk to him about the things that were deeper and more challenging in our lives. Pastor Ron had an ease about him, and many fellow students who were not religious came to have a deeper appreciation of faith because of Pastor Ron.

This day in chapel was one of the special chapels of the year. It was the annual awards chapel where we gave thanks to God for all the blessings that we received through the school year. Awards were handed out to students who excelled in certain areas. The highest award given out at LuHi each year was called the *Pro Deo et Schola* award (from the Latin meaning *For God and School*) This award was handed out each year to a graduating male and female senior who left their mark the most on the school in regards to serving others in faith and promoting the mission of the school. The recipients of this award would have their names engraved on a plaque in the entrance hallway of the school for the rest of the school's history. It was a common discussion in the senior hallway in the days leading up to the awards chapel that the award should go to me or to Tom Covington. Tom was the captain of the football team, was regularly in the local newspapers for his achievements, and was on his way to playing football for Georgia Tech on a full scholarship. Admittedly, I deeply desired that award. I felt that I deserved it because of all the chapels that I had led with Pastor Ron and all the other social ministry type of efforts I volunteered in over the years. And on a deeper level, the idea of having my name emblazoned on the wall for everyone to see as they entered the school would help to compensate for the deep pain and insecurity that I covered up because of everything revolving around my family.

When Tom's name was read at the chapel as the recipient of the *Pro Deo et Schola* award, I was devastated. I felt betrayed, and I felt like a failure. Yet God knows what is best for us, and what God did was right. Tom deserved the award more than me. Through the athletic skill that God had given to him, Tom was able to promote the school via avenues that were not open to me. Also, Tom was, and still is to this day, a man of great faith that shows itself in his love for others.

I needed this lesson in my life on my journey to Holy Ministry. It would be the first of many lessons that serving Jesus and the Church is not a life of awards and recognition. It is exactly the opposite. It is a life of humility and service. It is a life of sacrifice, often taking on and dealing with the hurts, pains, and consequences of those whom God calls us to serve. As I would continue my training and journey to ordination, this lesson would become clear to me, over and over again.

By the time I graduated LuHi, I knew that I wanted to study to be a pastor. Through many hours of deep discussion with Pastor Ron and my home pastor and many of the other blessed and selfless teachers and staff who served at Lutheran High School, I was able to work through my thoughts and fears and come to a decision to pursue this path to see if it was truly God's will for my life.

Up until April of my senior year, I was intent on attending Valparaiso University, the largest Lutheran college in the United States, located in the northwest corner of Indiana, about one hour from Chicago. But, as the time came closer to my leaving the house and going away to college, my parents balked and piled upon me heavy guilt about leaving them when I knew they needed my help in taking care of them in their sickness. At the last minute, I changed my intentions and enrolled in Concordia College in Bronxville, New York. Bronxville at the time was the "richest square mile in America," because it housed many bigwigs who worked on Wall Street. It was more nationally known for–and this was part of the tour for a prospective student– having the mansion that was filmed as the outside of Wayne Manor for the campy *Batman* television series of the 1960s.

Concordia Bronxville was a very small Lutheran college that was part of a system of Lutheran Colleges called "Concordias" spread throughout the country. It was located in Westchester County, New York. With light traffic, I could get home to Mom and Dad in an hour. Getting home to my parents was so important to them that they were able to persuade the college administration to make an exception to the rule that only juniors and seniors could have a car on campus. As a new freshman, I had my 1977 ugly light blue AMC Pacer on campus. My father gave the car the CB handle, the "blue bubble." It was more trouble than it was worth and having to leave every weekend did not help me and my attitude towards college. I think my English teacher at LuHi knew this could happen because when I told her about my change in direction regarding college, she told me that Concordia was not the best choice for me. Those words would echo in my head over the next four years.

When I attended Concordia, from 1987 to 1991, there were less than a thousand students. Half of the students were local commuters. About twenty percent of the school was Lutheran by religion. When I started that fall, I enrolled in the pre-seminary program. This program was in addition to your declared major (mine was behavioral science) that took the student through Biblical Greek and Hebrew, Lutheran doctrine courses, as well as other biblical studies in preparation for the seminary. For pastoral students who follow a traditional path to Holy Ministry, students would gain a bachelor's undergraduate degree and then go on to four more years at a seminary, which included a one-year internship at a church, to receive a Master's of Divinity. Nowadays, to meet the ever-changing needs of the church in this multicultural, nomadic world, there are several other nontraditional paths that someone who feels called to ministry could evaluate and pursue.

My four years of college were a mixture of personal trainwreck interrupted by God's grace and mercy. Once I got away from my parents and away from all of the daily responsibilities that they demanded of me, I decided that I would do as little as possible to get by. For instance, my mother sent me to college with seven towels, one for each day of the week, thinking that I would do wash every week. Well, after all those years of doing the wash for the entire family, those seven towels were seven weeks of showers. Of course, not having stringent restrictions and the incessant need for my parents to know where I was every minute of time, along with having a car on campus, I went wild with the freedoms! I drove anyone and everyone wherever they wanted to go. We went to the city, to the movies, to the bars, and out at two in the morning for pizza. About halfway through my freshman year, I told my parents that I had too much school work to continue coming home on weekends and came home less and less. Regrettably, this put more and more pressure on my sister, because she had to carry the brunt of the dysfunction during her first years in high school. It would have been a better use of my time had I really studied on those weekends, but no. I was not telling my parents the truth at that time. The weekends just offered more time for partying, dating, and sleeping.

I just barely graduated in four years from Concordia. I think my cumulative grade point average was a 2.3. My heart just was not in most of my classes. I did enjoy and got a lot out of my pre-seminary classes. For me, they served the purpose of what my future was going to look like. I had a hard time with the languages of Greek and Hebrew but got along enough with them. I also enjoyed my psychology and sociology classes, but they often hit a little too close to home regarding my life and family. I couldn't care less about any other classes that I needed to take for a "liberal arts" education, and my effort and grades reflected that reality.

The one good thing that would come of my time at Concordia was meeting and marrying my first wife, Linda, who would be the mother of my three children. Linda was, without a doubt, the prettiest woman on campus; but she was not a student there. Linda had graduated from Concordia two years before I started attending, so as you do the math, Linda was almost seven years older than me. When we met, she was the assistant to the dean of students in charge of student activities. She organized all the fun and social events for the students at the college, so she spent a lot of time with students.

When we met, I was immediately drawn to not only her beauty but to her caring heart and her family. As we got to know each other, we spent a lot of time with her family. Compared to my family, her family was great and normal. We would go to her home and have dinner together which included great conversation about the world and faith. We often went to family gatherings at state parks and other locations. This was a whole new world for me, coming from the darkness and isolation that had been my life. Linda was deeply religious. She studied to be a teacher and she loved children. For me, at twenty years old, she fulfilled all the ideas and expectations that I had for a relationship at that time in my life.

After a year and a half of dating, in the summer after I graduated from Concordia, we were married. We packed up everything we owned and set off for Fort Wayne, Indiana, where I would receive my seminary education.

During the course of my life and ministry, I have come to truly believe that God puts the right people in our lives at the right time. I have seen this happen over and over again. I believe that it is God's way of putting His hand around people to help nudge us along in the ways that we need to go. My journey to the seminary is another of these examples.

Not long after I graduated from high school, Pastor Ron left LuHi and took the call to be the pastor of St. James Lutheran Church in New Haven, Indiana, a suburb of Fort Wayne. He served there while I was at college. When nearing the end of your pre-seminary training, you need to decide which seminary will be the next step in your theological training. For the persuasion of Lutheran that I was at that time, there were two seminaries to choose from. There was a seminary in St. Louis and the one I attended in Fort Wayne. Pastor Ron and I had kept in touch over the years of college and, as it turned out, just as I was planning on attending the seminary, Pastor Ron was buying a house and moving out of the place he was renting. This was one of those times when the hand of God was clasped around me. The whole move to a new state became much easier and less stressful because Pastor Ron made arrangements for Linda and me to move into his apartment. I would also work with Pastor Ron at his church for the first few months that I was in Indiana until it was no longer permitted. More on that later when I discuss the differences among Lutherans.

My demeanor regarding seminary was much different from when I went to Concordia. This was it; I was finally fully immersed in what God was calling me to do. I put everything I could into my studies. I immediately found a church where I could not only do my fieldwork but also go above and beyond by helping with the youth group and other congregational activities. I found a bartending job at the Fort Wayne Coliseum that fit into my schedule. It would take a few months for Linda to find a permanent job, so we had a little more time on our hands as newlyweds; and by Christmas of that first year of our marriage, we were surprised to learn that we were expecting our first child, who would be Harrison. In a short period of time, we met, we dated, we got married, we moved halfway across the country, we set off officially for a church work career, and we started a family.

My years at the seminary were exceptional. I had great professors, and I am thankful for the education that I received. In addition to the seminary, I made sure that I was able to get as much practical experience as possible by preaching at local churches. As soon as I completed my preaching courses, I was allowed to take preaching assignments in Indiana and Ohio. I would get paid a little money while gaining more and more valuable experience. At least once a month during my time at the seminary, I drove an hour or two to churches where I could fill in and preach while the pastor was away. One weekend I drove all the way to Chicago, three hours from Fort Wayne, in a snowstorm to preach at a church. We used it as an extended weekend vacation and went to the Chicago Zoo.

At the time I attended seminary, the third year was the internship year. I was assigned my vicarage (as it is called in our tradition) in Long Island's North Fork at Our Redeemer Lutheran Church, Aquebogue, New York. By God's grace, I was back in New York where it was much more comfortable and more my style. But this would also bring me closer to my parents and everything that entailed.

My internship year was so successful that arrangements were made for me to quickly finish my final year of studies at the seminary and come back to be the associate pastor. With the finish line in sight after spending twenty-one of the first twenty-five years of my life as a student, I accelerated my classes by increasing my course load and graduated from the seminary in February 1995 so that I could return and be ordained as a pastor at the beginning of Lent. On March 12, 1995, through the laying on of hands by my bishop and others, the pastor's stole was placed around my neck, and I was ordained into the Office of the Holy Ministry.

I spent a total of three-and-a-half years at Our Redeemer, as both vicar and associate pastor, with mixed results. As soon as I came back as the associate pastor, we were blessed to welcome our second child, Samantha. We made friends who are still part of my life thirty years later. I learned a lot during my time there; but unfortunately, it was usually by doing the opposite of the senior pastor. Sadly, he was tired and burned out and needed a change, and it was obvious to many in the church. Half the church wanted the pastor, who had been there for seventeen years to leave. They would end up using me as the tool to achieve this goal. I was too young and inexperienced and was dealing too much with my own baggage to recognize the division and dysfunction going on in that church. Instead of being the calming force that I should have been, I listened to the accolades that fed me and became the catalyst for both of us leaving the church and moving on to other ministries. This was another valuable lesson about what it means to be a pastor.

Nonetheless, God worked through that experience, and every step of the journey, and through many blessed people, like Pastor Ron and others along the way who helped me to understand on a deeper level the gift of faith and the church. For each step and misstep in the process, the hand of God would be grasped around me through the sanctuary that is the church; and by God's grace, I would get to where God needed me to go.

Having finished my tenure at Our Redeemer in December 1996, I was called to St. John's Lutheran Church, Sayville. Those next eleven years would be the most important, challenging, and transformative years of my life.

Chapter 6
The Perfect Family Picture

The word *expectation* is one of the most dangerous words in the English language. Life is filled with expectations. From the time we are little, we are asked what we want to be when we grow up. We move through our formative years conjuring up images of what we think our future and our lives will look like. We enter into careers and relationships with predetermined pictures of what those things are going to be and bring to us. More often than not, what we expect in life is completely different from the reality.

The journey into Holy Ministry is no different. As I moved through high school, college, and seminary, I had pictures and expectations for my life and ministry that were formed not only by myself and my family but also by the culture and experiences in the church and the world around me. From what I had seen from my home pastor, it appeared that most of ministry was about leading church in fancy robes while beautiful music was played. There were meetings and the occasional hospital visit. There were potluck dinners and fun social events, as well as Bible studies and, of course, a lot of praying. But I would soon find out that the heart and soul of Holy Ministry was in the midst of heartache, tragedy, and getting "down and dirty" in the midst of the lives of the people a pastor is called to serve.

As a potential pastor journeys through the process of becoming a pastor, there are clear expectations placed upon the pastor and his or her family, and rightly so. While at the seminary, optional classes for pastors' spouses helped them know what to expect, as well as to understand how to act. As my life unfolded on the way to ministry, my personal expectations were compounded by the dysfunctional chaos that was my family of origin. As I went through college, dating, and looking for a mate, I had a clearly defined list of expectations of what my wife, my family, and my future would look like. Well, expectations in life have a funny (and not so funny) way of turning out, when the reality of sin and brokenness are in play!

When I was installed to be the sole pastor of St. John Lutheran Church, Sayville, New York on January 4, 1997, my life and ministry were unfolding exactly as I had hoped and expected. We had our two children and now, during my favorite time of year, Christmas, I was officially beginning to serve as the sole pastor of my own church. I was welcomed with open and eager arms by the new congregation. They had been deeply scarred by their experiences with my predecessor. In a little over six years, his leadership managed to cut the church's attendance in half and the finances along with it. There were stories of parishioners who were deeply affected by irrational, emotional outbreaks on the part of the pastor. The church needed the healing and energy that a new pastor with a young family would bring.

Under normal circumstances, a church like St. John's, Sayville, would never have taken the chance on a "wet-behind-the-ears" twenty-seven-year-old pastor. But, like so many of the chapters of my life, coming to St. John's was more of a gradual process than a clearly defined event with a designated starting line. When the prior pastor of St. John's finally succumbed to the wishes of the church and the bishop and moved on to another church in New Jersey, they found themselves quickly in need of a pastor's help in leading special services, conducting weddings, counseling in emergencies, and being present at leadership meetings. Because the church I was serving in Aquebogue had two full-time pastors, I was tapped to help at St. John's in the aftermath of their forcing their pastor to leave. By having the chance to get to know me over those summer months, because I was tasked with substituting in many pastoral acts, the congregation came to trust me and to see the potential that existed for our work together in the community. There was also hopeful excitement because 1997 was the hundredth anniversary of the church. There was an enthusiasm and energy that desired to celebrate the past while dreaming about a better future.

Those first years of ministry and family building kept us busy. I had one day off a week, and in an effort to be better than my father's voice in my head, I often used those Mondays off to renovate and repair things in the parsonage. (The church-owned house where we lived.) I was determined to make things a nice, pretty picture and comfortable place for my family. We raised the children, went on vacation, and tried to squeeze in all the things that my family never did.

In my second year at St. John's, July 1998, we welcomed our third child, Hunter, and decided that our family was complete. Yet, though everything was going as I dreamed and expected, the lurking darkness of family brokenness and dysfunction was creeping ever closer, soon to interrupt the perfect family pictures that we were desperately trying to paint.

In the time that I had served at Our Redeemer, Aquebogue before I came to Sayville, the situation regarding my parents had further deteriorated. Just as I was returning to Our Redeemer after finishing the seminary, my parents finally lost the financial battle regarding their house. They had no more relatives from whom they could coerce money; my childhood home was foreclosed. In my desire to be a good son, and do what would be expected of the pastor, I rallied all the help I could get to find them a place to live close to my first church and move them into it. On my days off, I would go over to their house and cut their lawn and help them out, while doing the same thing at my own home. But not long after they moved in, things exploded. What I did for them was never good enough or the way they wanted it done. They also continued to exist in their drug-clouded reality. Within a few months of moving into this rented house, they decided that they needed to get an old used church organ, which didn't work anymore, from a church that was closing in Connecticut. My father found the energy to rent a U-Haul® truck and hire two men to go with him to pick it up. The organ was so big that when it was being moved into the house, not only did the front door have to be removed, but also the door frame with it. The organ was placed into a room off the living room, where it sat the way it was left on the day it was brought in until they moved out of the house.

Things really came to a head with my parents when one night after Bible study at Our Redeemer, my father came up to the church and started screaming at me in the church entrance because of the way that I had mowed their lawn. It was at that moment that I began to pull away and informally begin the process of distancing myself from my parents. The reality was setting in that reasoning with them and treating them like rational people was impossible.

By the time Hunter was born, while we were at St. John's, Sayville, there was little communication with my parents. At the time that I was transitioning to my new church, my grandmother on my father's side was growing increasingly ill due to chronic obstructive pulmonary disease and emphysema. My Aunt Carolee, who now lived in Arizona, was trying to get my grandmother to move from Long Island to Sedona so that she could help care for her. This led to an intensification of triangling in the relationships within the family dynamic. *Triangling* is when people bring other people or circumstances into an existing strained relationship in the hopes of obtaining a favorable resolution. It's like when two siblings are fighting over an issue and one of the siblings goes and grabs a third sibling, not involved in the conflict, to obtain an ally that will win the argument. For my grandmother, this was a normal way of living life. She could not have a good relationship with both her son and her daughter at the same time. She often played situations and emotions off each of them to get her way. As her health deteriorated, her tendency to triangulate increased in her relationship with her children.

This led my grandmother, in the course of a year, to go from trying to live in Arizona to then letting my parents move in with her so they could "take care of her" (more of that manipulative, delusional thinking). The reality was that they could no longer afford to live in the rented house. They moved all of their stuff (junk really) into my grandmother's basement. Within weeks of moving into my grandmother's house, they managed to convince my grandmother to move out of her bedroom of fifty-plus years and give them the bedroom. This sad episode would only end after my grandmother hired her lawyer to pay my parents to move to Pennsylvania. When my grandmother died in November 1999, my Aunt Carolee had to itemize every single item in my grandmother's house, because of my father's delusional behavior and threats to pursue legal action, before we could liquidate the estate. My father could find all that energy needed to harass us in the aftermath of his mother's death, but he could not even bother to come to his mother's wake or funeral service.

In the meantime, all these family issues worked their way into my new calling in Sayville. Two months after Hunter was born, in one of their drug-induced tirades, my parents called the church in the middle of the night and left messages on the church's answering machine threatening to take my wife and me to court so that they could have visitation rights with their grandchildren. They even went as far as saying that we were unfit parents and they threatened to take our children away. When my office manager came in the next morning, she heard these messages. She was not only shocked but filled with fears regarding her own safety. This was the proverbial line in the sand. I reached out to a member of the church who was a lawyer, and after much painful consultation, I went to court to obtain a restraining order against my parents.

For many years following this episode, in my anger and embarrassment, I would hide and dance around any questions regarding my parents. The pastor's perfect family picture was cracked and shattered. I hated preaching on both Mother's and Father's Day. I felt like a fraud and a failure. After all, the fourth commandment is "Honor your mother and father". In my head, this certainly did not feel like I was keeping the Fourth Commandment.

While all this was going on, things with my wife's parents were also becoming strained. When Linda was thirteen years old, her birth parents went through a very bad divorce. Linda is the oldest of four children. She has three younger brothers. As the divorce was unfolding, Linda's mother decided to take the four children and, behind their father's back, move them from New York to Arizona. In effect, Linda's mother kidnapped her four children. Linda's father would eventually have to hire a private detective to hunt them down.

During the time her mother had them in Arizona, chaos reigned. The children were often left to fend for themselves. As the oldest, Linda became the mother to the younger brothers. Linda's next-oldest brother would often shoplift and get into trouble. One day, he set the neighbor's yard on fire.

Once Linda's father located the children, he spent a few days observing them to see how they were living. When the reality of the situation became clear, he came with the authorities to their school and took them back. They would not see their mother again for over ten years.

The emotional impact of this on Linda and her brothers cannot be overstated. When deep, traumatic, issues strike during childhood and formative years, there can often be an emotional stunting that occurs. The pain of the trauma is so immense that it is easier and safer for the person who has been hurt to avoid and detach from feeling too much. I believe that, for Linda and her family, this was the case in many ways. It was easier to just be in the moment and paint pretty pictures. It was difficult to discuss challenging issues. It was better to be busy and constantly doing something than to have to sit in the midst of the emotions and the realities that life often brought forth.

This would increasingly become an issue in our marriage. The deeper my ministry pulled me into the pain and crisis of other people's lives, the further detached, intimately and emotionally, we became from each other. While we were attracted to each other amid our own families' pain, it would be that pain that would work its way into our relationship and begin to push us apart.

There were also other dynamics surrounding Linda's family that would play out during this time. When our first son, Harrison, was born, I chose my only sibling, my sister, to be the godmother. Linda chose her oldest brother to be the godfather. On our first anniversary, Harrison was baptized at the church in Indiana where I was serving my fieldwork. My sister and Linda's brother, along with much of the rest of the family, traveled to Indiana for the baptism. During the course of that blessed weekend, we joked, "Wouldn't it be funny if the godparents, hooked up and got married." Well, five years later, the joke became the reality.

The connection and closeness that the four of us shared was a wonderful blessing, until it wasn't. We shared every holiday together. We went on vacations together. I spent countless days and weeks helping them renovate each house that they bought (and learned a lot in the process). We rejoiced with each child that was born. They eventually gave birth to two girls. Our five children share the exact same gene pool. My sister and I, along with our spouses, were desperately trying to create the family connections that didn't exist in our nuclear families. This would all be a great and worthy fantasy until my marriage fell apart.

Though the four of us shared a deep closeness as siblings, this closeness did not permeate Linda's entire family. Linda's father remarried a few years after the divorce from Linda's mother had settled when Linda was sixteen years old (before we met). His new wife brought a boy and a girl into the family. Linda's family was often referred to as the "Brady Bunch" because the family had grown to six children in total.

I remember that when I first started dating Linda and went to her parent's house, there was a big picture of all six family members hanging over the stairs as you entered the house. It was the perfect family picture. But sadly, much of keeping that family together was about the pictures and the expectations, not managing the reality of situations as they encountered them. When conflict arose in the family, especially among the siblings on the different sides of the parents, issues were dealt with in a way that did not lead to resolution. Instead, the parents would manage and manipulate the situation so that the two sides would no longer be exposed to the situation that created the issue. It was easier to cover up and avoid than to call it out and address it.

A big part of painting the family pictures was the need for the family to be together on the holidays. As a pastor who worked almost every single holiday, this would become a huge source of tension and conflict in our relationship. The last thing I (and most pastors) want to do on Christmas or Easter, after having conducted numerous liturgies in the preceding hours and days, is to get in the car and travel anywhere. Pastors are drained and exhausted, in a good way, when we finish our work on the "holy days." What energy we have left we want to spend with those who are close to us in a place where we can be comfortable and not have the pressure of expectations. This was so important to me when my children were younger that we made special arrangements with Santa Claus that our house would be his last stop before returning to the North Pole. While I was leading my last service on Christmas Day, Santa would come by our house. That way, the family had my undivided attention for the rest of the day to celebrate and play.

Linda's parents had some traditional expectations when it came to family, especially on holidays. Because their parents had expected them to always travel to them for special occasions, Linda's parents held the same belief regarding their children. They often tried to manage the stepchildren dynamics of the family in the same manner a traditional family would come together. Painting a cohesive family picture for the holidays was an important aspect of this.

On one of my first Thanksgivings as a pastor, after leading the Thanksgiving morning service, we set out in the car to travel to Linda's parents' house. We sat on the Throggs Neck Bridge, which connects Queens to Brooklyn, for two hours. It took us almost four hours to get to their house when it should have taken less than an hour and a half. Never again, I swore, was I traveling on the holidays after church. From that day forward, my household family would become accustomed to celebrating holidays in the days following the actual date.

This would become a major point of contention in my relationship with Linda's parents. They made an issue of being together for those big holidays and special occasions, but when it came to those more intimate and important moments of life, such as the grandchildren's school and sporting events, they were never around. Their lack of reciprocity for our life, my job, and our schedule made me feel like they never truly respected and understood what I did as a pastor. As the years passed on, the rift in the family, not just with me and Linda, but also with my sister and Linda's brother, as well as the stepsiblings, would continue to grow.

All of this family dysfunction would only further compound the loneliness that is a common characteristic of serving in the church as a pastor. While pastors and priests are called to care for, love, and be a friend to everyone whom they are called to serve, effectively and faithfully serving the people also requires strong and important boundaries. Pastors know and care for a lot of people, but often need to avoid getting too close to people. It's important for pastors to have friends and relationships outside of the church, but because of the demands of the calling, this is often impossible to do. If a pastor gets too friendly with certain people from the church, other parishioners become jealous. Though it is unfair, the perceptions of the pastor's relationships impact the pastor's ability to minister effectively to the community in which they serve.

The increasing intrusion of the troubles rooted in our families of origin into my own life and ministry, along with the natural loneliness of ministry, would bear down upon me as I moved through my work at St. John's, Sayville. From a professional perspective, my ministry was widely successful. The church was growing. We had programs for God's people of all ages. We were partnering with social ministries in the community, and the church increasingly had a good reputation in the community for being there for people when it was needed. For five years, I had my own pastoral interns, who were learning about ministry from me and the church. By the end of my eleven years there, the church had grown enough that one of those interns would be called back to be our Associate Pastor. My ministry was blessed and impactful. But, from a personal perspective, the success of my ministry at St. John's came at a heavy price.

Chapter 7
I Didn't Learn This in Seminary

It was the evening of July 17, 1996, and I was driving east on Sunrise Highway, the main east-west route on the southern shore of Long Island. I had just completed an appointment with a couple from St. John's Lutheran Church, Sayville, who were soon to be married. I was not yet the pastor of St. John's, because this was the summer when I was helping them out before they would call me to officially become their pastor.

As I was driving back home to Riverhead passing the William Floyd Parkway, a north-south connecting route, I saw fire engine after fire engine and ambulance after ambulance, klaxons blaring, racing by in the opposite direction. I have never in my life seen this number of rescue vehicles all seemingly heading to the same place. By the time I reached home, after nine in the evening, the news was beginning to break that TWA Flight 800 had come crashing as a fiery ball into the Atlantic Ocean just off Smith Point Beach on the south shore of Long Island.

A friend and colleague at a neighboring church who was a paramedic and a chaplain for the East Moriches Ambulance Company was among the early first responders on the scene. In the months that followed, I would meet regularly for lunch with this pastor and listen to him share the stories of heartache and pain that he witnessed and ministered to in the hours and days following this tragic plane crash. What he saw and witnessed on the waters and shore in those early hours had deeply and adversely affected my friend and colleague. He would spend countless months in therapy dealing with the trauma of seeing body parts, children's toys, and luggage floating in the waters of the Atlantic Ocean. As a chaplain, called to pray with and for his fellow first responders, he also had to deal with sharing their painful emotions and burdens.

In time, several years as a matter of fact, his heartache, trauma, and pain from those hours would be turned to good as he went on to become a certified emergency response counselor to others in the aftermath of headline news-making events. That role in his ministry would become extremely important five years later on September 11, 2001, when he would help many of those who went to Ground Zero deal with their grief.

As a pastor who had only been ordained a little over a year before, those stories that we shared over several lunches would ominously foreshadow similar emotions and struggles that I would experience in the years ahead. For my ministry would be nothing like the picture that I had made up in my head or had prepared for in my education.

The education that a future pastor receives at the seminary does a great job of helping us learn how to read and understand the Bible. Seminary professors teach how to conduct liturgical church services and how to understand the significance of the ritual and symbolism. Of course, doctrinal understanding is at the heart of seminary training. For Lutheran pastors, understanding the concepts of Law (God's commandments and instructions for our lives) and Gospel (the good news of God's grace, love, and forgiveness in Jesus' death and resurrection) are at the heart of all our theological training. But moving from the theory of the classroom and chapel to the real dirt and mess of everyday life is not the primary function of religious seminaries. It is hoped that the one year in an internship before graduation from seminary will prepare a potential pastor for what is yet to come.

Over the course of my ministry, I have come to believe that no amount of classroom time at the seminary can ever truly prepare for what a pastor, who really cares for and spends time with their people, will come to see, smell, touch, and experience. I should have had a clue about this when my pastor showed up at our home during the trauma with our grandfather, but I was too young to put it together.

In my eleven years of service at St. John's, Sayville, I was called upon to give pastoral care in the midst of several situations that made it to the front page of the newspaper. I ministered to people in situations that I would have thought came directly from a Hollywood soap opera script. To this day, in over fifteen years more of ministry since I parted from Sayville, I have not been called to minister in similar situations of the same intensity. The stories I share in this chapter are just a few of those intense pastoral care moments.

It was the Tuesday in Holy Week 2000. Holy Week is the most important week of the year for Christians. It starts on Palm Sunday, where Jesus's entrance into Jerusalem is observed. The week then moves through the various important moments in those last days before Jesus would die on the cross and subsequently rise on Easter morning. Many churches, including mine at St. John's, hold a service each day from Palm Sunday to the following Easter Sunday.

Amid the nonstop obligations of Holy Week, I came home for a quick dinner on that Tuesday night, April 18. I wanted to spend a quick hour or so with the family. Harrison was eight, Samantha was five, and Hunter was two. As I picked up my fork to dig into the first few bites of dinner, the phone rang. It was the Episcopal Priest, who was a fire department chaplain, asking me to immediately come down to the Sayville

Long Island Railroad train station. Jennifer, a seventeen-year-old high school student, whom I had confirmed into the Christian faith during my first year at St. John's, had just jumped in front of the train, killing herself because her boyfriend broke up with her.

I arrived at the train station just a few minutes after her mother and found her mother sitting on the bumper of the ambulance. Her mother wanted to see Jennifer. She needed confirmation that it was her daughter. She was having a hard time believing and accepting that it was true. The emergency responders, however, were not going to allow Jennifer's mother, or anyone else, near the site of the accident.

In the days that followed, I spent a lot of time with Jennifer's family and at the high school where Jennifer was a student. In those hours with Jennifer's family, the nagging need to be sure that it was Jennifer, and to determine whether or not the casket could be open for the funeral, was the obsession of Jennifer's mom. In my deep desire to help and try to bring comfort to this family, I offered to Jennifer's mom that I go into the funeral home, with the funeral director, with whom I had a good relationship, and see Jennifer's body and share my thoughts with the family regarding how to proceed with the funeral.

I did not realize what I was offering to do and how what I would see would impact me. Jennifer's upper body and head bore the brunt of the collision with the train. She did not at all look like the girl whose head I placed my hand on a few years earlier to bless at her confirmation. It was hard to recognize her at all. To this day, I can vividly see in my mind's eye what I saw when I walked into the prep room at the funeral home.

I advised Jennifer's family that a closed casket would be appropriate for the visitation at the funeral home. They decided however, that they too wanted to see Jennifer and they wanted her high school friends to understand the impact that suicide has on the family left behind. The funeral home did the best it could to piece together and prepare Jennifer for viewing, but the end product was a powerful reminder that death is the ugly result of this imperfect, broken world.

Jennifer's funeral was held in St. John's sanctuary on the Saturday between Good Friday and Easter Sunday. In my opinion, Easter Saturday is one of the best days of the year to hold a funeral, for the day itself figuratively represents exactly what death is for us who look to Christ as our hope and resurrection. Our death and burial is that time in between while we wait to rise with Jesus. Easter Saturday is a day of waiting for Christians between the sadness and death of Good Friday and the joy and triumph of Easter morning.

For a long time, Christian churches refused to bury suicide victims from the church. The reasoning behind this refusal was connected to the idea that people who kill themselves end their lives in a state of sin, with no chance to repent. Thankfully, this mentality has changed in recent history. For if the population of heaven is determined by having to die in a perfect state of grace and perfection, then heaven is going to be a very empty place! If there is ever a time when the message of God's grace and love is needed, it is when a family is utterly devastated and destroyed because a loved one's life was so overwhelmed by the effects of sin and brokenness that they lost all hope and gave up. My message to Jennifer's family on that Easter Saturday was that the world is too often filled with moments that leave us speechless and reaching for something to say. It's in those moments that God reaches out to us, especially with the grace of baptism, where God assures us that God is with us always. At the end of the sermon, I pleaded with the many teenagers in attendance to never allow their struggles and problems to prevent them from reaching out to a pastor, priest, parent, or friend to find help.

As I dropped off Harrison and Samantha at their elementary school on September 11, 2001, I had been listening to the New York all-news radio station, 1010 WINS. When I was sitting in the line of cars waiting to pull up to the drop-off zone, the news was just beginning to break that a plane had crashed into the north tower of the World Trade Center. As I left the school zone and headed to the church, there was much speculation as to whether it was a small commuter plane. Within minutes of reaching the church, the phones started ringing as now people were calling to tell us that the south tower had also been hit. At this point, I headed over to my intern's house, which was across the street from the church, and I watched the news unfold on the television. As we stood in stunned silence and watched each tower collapse, I had the horrible sinking feeling that our church and the Sayville community would not go untouched by the events of this day.

Indeed, the small community of Sayville, about an hour's drive from Manhattan, had eleven funerals for residents of the community in the weeks following September 11. There were candlelight vigils at many of the houses of those victims. There was an ecumenical prayer service held in the center of town ten days later. I shared a meditation alongside most of the other religious leaders of the community from Romans 8: 18-39, reminding the hundreds gathered that even when we are so overwhelmed that we don't know if we can pray, God's Spirit intercedes for us. It was the message that God does not abandon us in our most crucial hour of need.

It would take a few days for September 11 to personally come home to St. John's, Sayville. In those first few hours and days that followed, I made sure that I was constantly near my church office to take any calls. We held a Wednesday night prayer service in the sanctuary to speak to and pray for the tragedy. I left the church doors open all day for people to come and go to sit, meditate, and pray.

By the weekend after September 11, I began to breathe a sigh of relief that St John's did not have anyone personally taken in the moment of evil. But a few moments after the last Sunday service ended on September 16, my office phone rang. Firefighter John Napolitano, who served in the FDNY Rescue 2 division, had not come home. The family waited all week, hoping that he would walk through the door. Those immediate days after the event were chaotic in ways that were impossible to imagine. There was no cell service in or out of the city. The bridges were closed. Many people were fleeing the city in whatever ways possible to get away, while others were trying to get to the city to try to help. By Sunday, the reality sank in that John was not coming home.

John was married to Ann, and they had two very young daughters, Elizabeth and Emma. I baptized John's youngest daughter, Emma, less than two years before this event. We were not able to have the funeral until October 2. There were multiple funerals each day in those weeks and months following that dreadful Tuesday. The funerals were scheduled so that each first responder could have the appropriate turnout of uniformed service people as well as dignitaries who could speak and offer condolences at the funeral. Fire commissioner Thomas Von Essen attended the funeral at St. John's to offer New York Fire Department reflections.

Families also waited as long as they could, in the hopes that some human remains would be found. During this time, while ministering to John Napolitano's family, I came to truly understand how important the ritual of a funeral is in helping the survivors comprehend, accept, and begin to move forward from death, especially a tragic death. At the time that John's funeral was scheduled, his human remains had not been found. So important was it for the family to have something to bury and to move through the funeral process that they decided they would get a casket and fill the casket with John's uniform, favorite sports team memorabilia, and pictures and notes from the children and family. The casket then moved through the funeral process. People paying their respects filed past the casket in the funeral home. The casket was loaded onto the back of a firetruck and moved into the church. When the funeral service was over, the casket was placed back on top of the fire truck and slowly rolled less than a mile from the church to the cemetery where the casket would be placed. I rode with the casket, sitting in the front of the fire truck. We slowly paraded down Main Street in Sayville. Both sides of the street were lined with many people holding flags, making the sign of the cross, and bowing their heads in prayer as the firetruck and casket rolled by.

A weird mixture of emotions filled me during that short ride to the cemetery. Tears rolled down my face as the full impact of September 11 crashed down on me. It was the first moment in the weeks that I had been ministering to John's family that I let myself breathe and feel the moment. I was overwhelmed with the deep sadness that this had happened in our world, while at the same time, I felt a deep sense of humility that I was able to offer just a little bit of help and hope in the face of overwhelming, universal grief.

Surprisingly, the message that I offered at John's funeral was easy to write because John made it easy. It was shared with me before the funeral that John would often sign greeting cards he gave to family and friends by writing, "May the Lord hold you in the hollow of His hand." This was a gift from God as a theme to tie his funeral sermon together. I chose the hymn for the funeral, "Lord, Take My Hand and Lead Me," and I preached from the Isaiah 25 text that talks about God's hand "wiping every tear from our eyes" as well as using Jesus, as the Good Shepherd, as a backdrop to talk about protection from God exemplified through people like John, who offer their lives in protection for others. Every time I sing the hymn "Lord, Take My Hand and Lead Me," my thoughts turn to John Napolitano and September 11. The words of the second stanza that I quoted in John's Sermon, always bring me comfort: *Lord, when the tempest rages, I need not fear; For you, the Rock of ages, are always near. Close by your side abiding, I fear no foe, For when your hand is guiding, In peace I go.*

The first pastoral intern assigned to me while I was the pastor of St. John's was Vicar Karl, from Summer 1999 to Summer 2000. Karl was a late-twenties Naval Reservist who was newly married. As my first intern, Karl had a special place in my heart, and we fast came to be friends. During that year, when he was supposed to learn from me, I learned as much from him. It's one thing to do the work of a pastor. It's another to have to teach, explain, and rationalize why and what you are doing to someone who doesn't do the work each day and is eager to understand it all. Karl set a high standard for the four vicars who would follow him.

Not long after he finished his studies at the seminary and became a pastor, Karl was struggling in his marriage. Because we were still friends, we stayed in contact with each other, often connecting at professional pastoral gatherings. Due to the stress of his relationship, Karl and I had a falling out because of some misunderstood words related to his marriage. For over a year, we did not talk to each other.

In summer 2002, while in his early thirties, Karl, still married and now the father of two children, was diagnosed with terminal stomach cancer. One year later he was gone. In that time from his diagnosis to his funeral, Karl and I reconciled. We shared many reflections over our time together during his internship. His courage and faith as he was facing his mortality was inspirational for me.

We held a memorial service for Karl at St. John's a few weeks after his funeral. During that service, I had to wrestle with losing a friend so young while understanding Karl's place in my journey and ministry. This was another one of those moments when I again came to understand that ministry is most needed and most effective in the depths of the dirt and darkness of the world.

Glen joined St. John's around 2000. He owned a painting company and was eager to learn more about the faith and wanted to join in and help volunteer in whatever ways he could at the church. I quickly came to know Glen and his family. His wife was a pharmacist who was raised in Pakistan and practiced the Muslim faith. Prior to her marriage to Glen, she had been in an arranged marriage. She had three children from that marriage who became Glen's stepchildren. The stepchildren lived with Glen and their mother most of the time.

On June 25, 2004, the children's father came back to Glen's house to drop them off from visitation. After the father dropped the children and they went into the house, Glen and his wife were standing on the front steps. Upon seeing Glen with his ex-wife, the children's father floored his 2003 Toyota Highlander and ran Glen over, right in front of his wife. The car crashed into the fencing next to the house. He threw the car into reverse, most likely trying to finish the job, but the car had become stuck on the fence and could no longer move.

Though Glen survived the attack, he suffered horrific injuries to his pelvis and legs. He had a ruptured spleen and collapsed lungs. When I first arrived at the hospital, we did not know whether or not he would survive. Once the immediate crisis passed, Glen would spend the next eighteen months in a rehab facility healing, regaining his strength, and figuring out how to walk again on a leg that needed a brace to hold it steady.

I spent many hours visiting Glen in the rehab center over his months of recovery. It was very hard to see such a vibrant man struggle just to stand. Most of the people at the rehab center were twice Glen's age, which only compounded the emotional trauma that he was dealing with in the aftermath of the event. When Glen finally returned home, a special ramp and wheelchair were needed. But Glen eventually figured out how to walk again. Glen became a dear friend and huge inspiration to me and others during his time of recovery.

Nearly two years later, the ex-husband would go on trial for attempted murder. Throughout this time, his three children would continue to be cared and provided for by Glen and their mother. During the trial, I would come to the courtroom and sit in the observer's section to offer my moral support to Glen, especially during his testimony. It was heart-wrenching and extremely painful watching Glen testify and relive the moment. He spoke in clear detail about lying on the ground seeing the reverse lights come on, while the tires were spinning and digging up dirt, thinking to himself that he was about to die.

As the trial was concluding, on May 1, 2006, Glen's assailant jumped in front of a subway train and killed himself. There was no conclusion to the trial. There was no satisfaction for Glen with a guilty verdict and jail time. This also would further complicate any chance of a civil case moving forward for some type of restitution. On top of all of that, Glen now had to become the sole father figure to three very confused and hurting children left behind.

Despite the setback, Glen would not allow this event to define his life or derail his spirit. He went on to join

Toastmasters, and won many awards as a public speaker, inspiring others with his story. For me personally, Glen would become a friend who, when my life came crashing apart years later, would give back to me what I had given to him.

January 2007 through January 2008 would offer to me the most challenging pastoral care moments of my ministry. In early January 2007, I received a call as the ambulance company chaplain to come to the hospital to assist a family dealing with the death of their seven-year-old boy. His mother found him unresponsive in his bed when they woke up that morning. When I entered the room in the emergency section of the hospital, the mother was leaning over her boy hugging him as tight as she could while she sobbed. I moved through a liturgy of scripture, comfort, and prayer and then just stood back at the side of the hospital bed, hoping my mere presence would offer comfort. As the time moved on, the mother lifted her head and through tear-filled eyes and in a broken voice said to me, "Please keep reading … please keep giving me hope …" I quickly opened up my Bible and kept moving from passage to passage that I could remember and find that would remind her, and all gathered in that small room, of the hope that Jesus gives in death. It was a reminder to me that it wasn't about me and what I could come up with to bring comfort. It was about God … and God's Word … and what God is doing to bring comfort in the face of sin and death.

Just a few months later, in April, it would happen again. This time, it was a four-year-old child of someone with whom I had a passing acquaintance in high school. It was another unexpected death of a child that had no immediate explanation.

In the aftermath of these two tragedies, I found myself

going home and standing over the beds of my own children, now fifteen, twelve, and nine, projecting the feelings and emotions of those families onto my own life. I also became even more painfully aware of how alone I felt in dealing with the tragedies that I ministered to and with the emotional baggage that came with them. My wife, Linda, was a kind-hearted, lovely person, but understanding and supporting pastoral care situations was not possible for her. The reality and pain of the emergencies that I was thrust into were never talked about at home. As I watched and ministered to the pain of others, I started reevaluating my own life's journey.

A month later, in May 2007, I would again be thrust into headline-making events. In May 2001, I placed my hand on the head of Matthew Baylis and confirmed him into the Christian faith. After the events of September 11, Matthew moved through high school with the desire and intention of serving his country in the military as soon as he graduated. And he did exactly that. Upon graduation from high school, he enlisted in the Army and eventually was sent overseas to serve in Iraq.

On May 31, 2007, Matthew was killed in Iraq ten days after his twentieth birthday. His commanding officer explained in a letter how he was killed in action:

> "It was a night mission in Baghdad. Matthew's squad was entering a courtyard of a known insurgent compound. The squad leader, the platoon leader and Specialist Baylis, carrying the squad automatic weapon, came under heavy fire. The platoon leader was hit. Matthew immediately laid down a base of fire allowing the other soldiers to retrieve their platoon leader and get to cover. Matthew was fatally hit while seeking cover after expending his 100 rounds from the [weapon's] magazine".

On June 9, 2007, the funeral was held in the sanctuary of St. John's. I preached from the Passion story of Jesus from John's Gospel where Jesus stood before Pontius Pilate and was questioned about his kingdom. Jesus reminded Pilate, and all who hear his words today, that His kingdom is not of this world. I used the picture of worldly kingdoms in conflict to point Matthew's family and friends toward the only kingdom that truly brings us the hope of peace.

As we exited the church to make our way to Calverton National Cemetery, not only were the news cameras present, but the front of the church was also surrounded by nearly a hundred bikers carrying American flags. There had been rumors that a radical, fundamentalist group who had been showing up at soldiers' funerals protesting the war were making their way to Matthew's funeral. These bikers made it their mission to stand in the way and shield the family and friends from any additional emotional trauma. Fortunately, the rumors turned out to be false, but the bikers' presence was a blessed reminder of what good can happen when people come together for the right reasons.

The occasion of Matt Baylis' funeral was another time of confused emotions. I was honored to have officiated over the funeral of a hero who lived out the call of Jesus by sacrificing his life for others. But I again was overwhelmed with the stark reality of the horrors of the world. This was a far cry from the pictures of ministry that I had painted in my head.

Seven months after Matt's funeral in January 2008, I would preside over the funeral of sixteen-year-old Russell. He was a tall, strong young man who had contracted a bacterial infection from a high school wrestling mat, through a tiny cut on his nose. He was hospitalized for over a month as the infection led to sepsis and eventually death. Russell had recently taken up boxing and loved the *Transformers* show and movies. I combined those two themes into his funeral sermon, talking about how, sometimes in this life, our faith struggles and fights with God to make sense of things, while God is at work through Jesus, transforming us from death to life.

Compassion Fatigue is an occupational hazard for those whose vocation is to help others in their time of need. When one empathizes with others during their trauma, there is the risk that one's own issues and emotions will be compromised. When one's own life or family is out of order or immersed in conflict or dysfunction, the ability to appropriately distance oneself emotionally and personally becomes challenging.

As my tenure at St. John's moved toward its conclusion, and my family's dysfunction came to its apex, I found myself wrestling personally with many things. I was dealing with issues that were not a regular part of pastoral ministry. I was not happy at home, feeling more alone when there were people home, than when I was home alone. I knew I was in trouble when I saw a cartoon in one of the Sunday newspaper magazines. It was a picture of Batman sitting on a therapist's couch. He was holding his head in his hands, and he said in the bubble above his head, "Who rescues me?!"

I spent so much time trying to live the perfect picture of life, trying not to be like my father while trying to save everyone else, that I sometimes forgot that I worked for the Savior. But I myself was NOT the savior, and I was not invincible. And sometimes you can only be rescued when you realize that everything is crashing.

Chapter 8
(Un)Faithful

"But how are you doing?"

"I'm fine," I replied.

But she asked again, "No, I mean, how are you really doing? How's your head? How are you sleeping at night, dealing with these things that you are dealing with?"

I replied, "No one has ever asked me that before ... no one has really cared about my feelings in all of this ...."

At that moment, I knew our relationship would be different and that I wanted her to be part of my life ... From. That. Day. Forward.

I first met Lisa when her daughter, Mackenzie, and my youngest son, Hunter, were in the four-year preschool class together in 2003 at St. John's. Lisa would first be made aware of who I was when Mackenzie came home from school one day and announced, "God came to school today." From there, Lisa asked around to the other mothers who this "god" was. He was not "god," he was me, the pastor. But this confusion is often made by preschool children.

Lisa was a bit of a celebrity around town because she grew up in Sayville and had gone on to marry the father of Melissa Joan Hart, the star of the Disney® show, *Sabrina the*

Teenage Witch. Wherever Lisa went, the whispers would quickly start, "Isn't that Melissa Joan Hart's stepmother?" Or for little Mackenzie, "Isn't she the sister of Melissa Joan Hart?" And yes, when I first heard about and eventually met Lisa at the St. John's Preschool, that is how she was identified to me.

In the year that followed our initial meeting, Lisa became part of a group of friends, outside of the church, that began to gather on a regular basis. We were all bonded by our children, who hit it off and created friendships that fed the adult get-togethers.

It was such a relief and a blessing for me to begin to expand my social circle outside the fellowship of the church. These were people who saw me merely as *Harry.* Not pastor. Not counselor. Not crisis care interventionist. I could be myself without fear of judgment. We would drink and laugh and hang out at the pool, while the children played "manhunt" and watched their favorite Disney® movies.

In time, our social gatherings were centered around the reality television show *Survivor.* Every Thursday at 8 p.m., we rotated through different houses and watched the show. The enthusiasm for this would greatly multiply during the Spring 2005 season, when Sayville's own Tom Westman, an FDNY fireman, not only competed on *Survivor* but ended up winning the whole thing. Tom's child attended the St. John's Preschool during the year his father was on the show. That season ended with the town of Sayville gathered under a tent in a park in the center of town watching the final episode, while CBS cameras recorded the live reaction of the community to Tom's being announced as the million-dollar winner.

Those *Survivor* Thursdays would become the backdrop to increasingly intense conversations between Lisa and me. At first during the commercials, then after each episode, and eventually, as the seasons went on, during the airing of the show itself – Lisa and I found ourselves talking more and more and more. Both our spouses were present during those evenings, but neither really took interest in the things we were talking about.

As time went on, I found that Lisa was filling a deep void in my life. There was no other person in the world with whom I could discuss the things that I talked about with Lisa. We discussed church issues, spiritual topics, politics, raising children, and all of the stupid mundane things in life, while constantly laughing. When Lisa was twenty-one, she spent a year traveling the world, experiencing amazing things, and taking in other cultures. She had a perspective in life that I had rarely encountered. Lisa is an artist who taught me how to pause more in life to notice the shadows, the details. She is whimsical and spontaneous, scattered, and amazingly equipped to roll with things. She is the exact opposite of me, and this balance was a refreshing refuge. As I dealt with each of the pastoral care crises outlined in the prior chapter, I found myself reaching out to Lisa, more and more, in the aftermath of each episode. I would vent to her and debrief, and just find a place where someone would listen and understand.

With my parents' illnesses leading to them turning against me and with my wife's unavailability to explore deeper emotional issues, Lisa was the first person in my life, who truly expressed care and concern for me and my well-being on a regular, personal basis. She remembered what was going on in my life, and when she didn't hear from me, she checked in.

I knew I was in trouble when one day I was looking at my cell phone bill and saw that Lisa's phone number vastly outnumbered all the other numbers I called, combined. Over the period when I buried those four children, the depth of the intimacy of my relationship with Lisa multiplied and plunged to places that I could have never imagined. What started as a friendship grew into an emotional affair that eventually did not stop there.

In my experience, personally and as a pastor, emotional affairs are as devastating, and maybe even more destructive, than mere physical affairs. In today's culture of loose sexual mores where open marriages, throuples, and swinging have become common, affairs based solely on sex are painful and destructive but, in my opinion, don't obliterate marriage with the same explosive force as emotional affairs. With physical affairs, there is a chance that, through hard work and forgiveness, the marriage can recover. It is not so easy with an emotional affair.

In an emotional affair, one of the spouses has made a conscious, intentional decision to go outside the marriage for all of the intimacies that should be the bedrock and foundation of the marriage. Emotional affairs are affairs of the heart that share all the things that make up healthy intimacy–spiritual, intellectual, relational, and emotional intimacy. Left unchecked, emotional affairs will culminate in the physical, and at that point, there is little hope left for the existing marriage. The spouse involved in the emotional affair has already left the marriage. It just hasn't been made official.

The cycle of sin in life is a tricky, slippery slope that is hard to identify at first. In my pastoral experience, I have learned that no one ever wakes up one day and announces, "I'm going to have an affair ..." or ... "I'm going to be an alcoholic ..." or "I'm going to become a kleptomaniac ..." The pathway of sin is like a slow leaking drip. At first, unnoticeable, then increases until it leads to drowning.

Never in my life did I think I would become unfaithful in my marriage. Never in my life did I think I would consciously make decisions that would lead to divorce. Never did I think that I would be willing to risk everything–my children, my career, my very soul–for something like this.

In January 2008, I took a trip by myself to Arizona to spend some time with Aunt Carolee and Uncle Bill. They were my emotional parental type go-to and support throughout my adulthood and time in the ministry. As I began to open up, but not totally, because I was embarrassed and still in my own sense of unbelief that my life had gotten to this place, they emphatically insisted that I had to tell my wife that the marriage was in deep trouble and that we go to counseling.

After I returned, Linda and I entered counseling together. It became clear very quickly that we had become two different people from who we were when we first married and that there wasn't much left emotionally for us to work with. My experiences as a pastor had forced me to mature and deal with real-world issues. She was perfectly content with living a simple, moment-by-moment, carefree life. The circumstances regarding the dysfunction passed on from our families also made it clear to me that I did not want to be in a relationship that was conflicted, unsupportive, and lacking full intimacy.

At one point during our counseling, the counselor met with me alone and said, "Harry, you have to decide what you are going to live with. Your wife is who she is, and she is not going to change." The pressure of that statement weighed on me and further fueled the dissolution of our relationship. For a long time, I had been feeling the pressure of being the pastor, the main parent, the planner and organizer of our home, the fixer, and now, the pressure of the future of the marriage was being placed on my shoulders. That statement drove home for me the loneliness of my life at that time.

I was in an unhappy marriage. Years of brokenness and dysfunction, compounded by the compassion fatigue of my ministry, had brought me to this place. Yet, though everything was falling apart, on a deeper level, I knew that my life could not continue to go the way it was going, painting perfect pictures of the perfect family and pastor, where everything was all right. And I had found in Lisa, the partner, the soulmate, the friend, I never had before.

In no way am I attempting to condone unfaithfulness, nor am I trying to justify my actions. Allowing myself to get to this point and to hurt Linda the way she was hurt was wrong, and I am deeply sorry for the pain I caused her (and yes, I have told her that). My hope in sharing the reality of this downfall is to further underscore how the destructive tug of sin works in our world and points to our need for God's gracious, loving, and guiding hand in our lives. It's a powerful object lesson when the pastor, who dedicates his life full time to doing God's work is not immune from such struggles.

On August 3, 2008, the day after what would have been my seventeenth wedding anniversary, I began a three-month leave of absence from St. John's, which would culminate with my resignation on November 4. The time during the leave of absence was used by the bishop to investigate the circumstances surrounding my marriage and my relationship with Lisa. A special investigator was appointed to meet with all the parties involved–church leaders, our spouses, Lisa, and me. The church took the situation very seriously, as they should have. The fact that Lisa was Melissa Joan Hart's stepmother further complicated things, as there was a very real danger of the church's experiencing a public relations nightmare. I knew during that time where all this was headed. It was embarrassing and humiliating. I said very little to the members of the church whom I had faithfully served for eleven years. I just needed to take care of myself and my children and begin the work of rebuilding my life, whatever that would look like.

I restarted counseling through the Lutheran Counseling

Center. They had been a helpful and affirming presence throughout my life and ministry, and the counselors there would again play an integral role in moving my life forward. For an interim period of time, I started working with a friend who was a carpenter, helping him renovate houses. It was a nice change of pace, working with my hands and body while letting my mind rest and work through all this. Most importantly, I went back home to my church in Amityville.

After twenty years of absence, I went back to the place that had helped to mold and nurture my faith. The pastor, not the pastor of my youth, but a colleague who was fully aware of the circumstances, welcomed me home. I would slip into the balcony of the church each week and sit there in the church and receive the gifts that God gives, gifts we so desperately need when sin and brokenness tear apart our lives. Some of the older members remembered me and were happy to have me back. Those services back home were powerful and another instrumental part of the healing that would take place in the aftermath of all these circumstances. Years later, I would get the opportunity to return the favor to that same pastor when he went through some painful personal struggles.

This is one of the most important messages from the Bible regarding God's grace. You can always go home to the sanctuary of the church. No matter who we are … no matter what the circumstances may be … God's goal is not to destroy us permanently, banish us eternally, or punish us unceasingly. God's goal is to pick us up, heal us, and rebuild our lives for the better, and for the service of God's kingdom.

Even when human beings judge one another and condemn each other, based upon their own opinions and interpretations of what they believe the Bible says, over and over again the true message of Scripture, seen in the death and resurrection of Jesus, is that God's heart breaks with us when we are broken, and God's desire is to heal us, save us, and get our lives straight again.

It was good, proper, and just that I no longer be allowed to continue serving as a pastor as a result of all this mess in my life. But thinking that I should be punished unceasingly, and condemned to hell eternally, runs counter to God's grace and to all the examples of the sinful, broken people that God used in the Bible for the sake of His work in the world. The Biblical stories of Moses, David, Jonah, the Apostles, Paul, and many others are the stories of God using sinful, imperfect, broken people for the sake of the Gospel.

Ultimately, the main point of the Bible is restoration and making a comeback. The horror, the defeat, and the sorrow of Jesus' death on the cross on Good Friday is not the end. The empty tomb and new life of Easter morning are why Jesus is the center and foundation of our faith.

Little did I know at that time that God would use this painful, confusing, and humbling episode in my life to teach me once again how God's grace really works in our world.

Chapter 9
Tales of The First Born Son

It was Labor Day weekend 2006. We had taken our camper out to Indian Island Campground for the last weekend of summer before the start of the new school year. Indian Island is in Riverhead at the beginning of the north fork of Long Island. It is a beautifully wooded campground that skirts the waters of the Peconic Bay, in between the north and south fork of the Island.

It was Sunday night and we were finishing our time around the campfire outside the camper. Hunter and Samantha had retired into the camper to watch a movie and fall asleep. Linda, Harrison, and I were sitting around the fire. Harrison was beginning high school in just a few days. In my ongoing effort to be *SuperDad* by being a better father than my father, I decided that this would be a good time to raise some serious conversation with Harrison.

In my best authoritative Dad voice, thinking I had a handle on all the subjects that could possibly be raised by a fourteen-year-old, I said, "So Harrison, you are about to enter into high school. You are probably going to hear about things that you may not understand or you may have questions about. I want you to know that you can come to me with anything, and I will do my best to answer you and help you. So, is there anything that you have any questions about?"

In my head, I was thinking that Harrison would ask something like, "What's a B.J.?" But without skipping a beat, Harrison asked me, "How does someone know if they are gay?"

Thank God it was dark out! Thank God my face was obscured by the smoke and the flames from the fire! The silence and shock in my head felt like it lasted a lifetime, but it was probably only a few seconds. I recovered quickly enough and answered something like, "These years will help you understand many things about who you are and your body." That would be the beginning of an incredible, life-changing journey, for both me and Harrison.

In the background of all the things I was dealing with that led to the revelation of the last chapter was the progressive struggle that Harrison was having regarding his sexuality. In truth and hindsight, I shouldn't have been so shocked when Harrison asked that question around the campfire. The clues and behaviors had been there since he was a little boy. But because of my position as a pastor in a church (at that time) that did not accept homosexuality and because it's the last thing that a father dreams of for his son, it was easier for me to repeatedly go into denial, rather than have to face the reality of another aspect of life that might shatter the perfect family picture.

I remember when I found out that we were expecting our first child. Immediately, I started dreaming up all the expectations I had for becoming a father. Because of all the things I wanted to do with my father but never got to do, I was immediately determined to do all those things with my son that my dad never did with me. As a result of this, I desperately desired that my first child be a boy. I was so eager and anxious to be SuperDad that my first child just *had* to be a boy. As we waited expectantly for the baby to come, we decided that for this child, our first, we did not want any gender revelations before the moment of birth. But deep down, I was praying hard for a boy.

One of the most powerful spiritual moments of my life

was watching Harrison, and then my other two children being born. It boggles my mind when a woman who has given birth to a child does not believe in God. The whole experience is just miraculous. The whole process is incredible. This microscopic, little protozoa-like cell hooks up with an egg and in nine months grows into this incredible little life that within a year is walking and talking and keeps on growing. Even though things in life can go wrong, so much is right in the way our arms, legs, and bodies all have things that work together so perfectly. Then that place where this miracle of life comes from goes back into shape so more babies can be made. I just cannot believe that this is some freak accident of nature. The miracle of life drives my search and understanding of the Divine.

At the moment of Harrison's birth, I was so wrapped up in the experience and then, as the baby came out, counting fingers and toes, that I completely forgot about my desire for a boy. Then, like in a distant vacuum, I thought I heard the doctor say, "It's a boy," and then I looked and saw that it was indeed true! We were off to the races, or shall I say, Yankees games, playing catch, fishing together, and doing *manly* things.

It was with the birth of Harrison that it was verified to me that God does indeed have a wicked sense of humor. Be careful what you pray for and expect when you ask God for something. For God does indeed hear our prayers, but often God gives answers to our prayers that are completely opposite of what we think we want and need.

The first time I took Harrison to a Yankees game in the Bronx, around the time he was four years old, he and his friend were more interested in the planes flying overhead than in anything happening on the field. The first time we played catch with a baseball, the ball hit Harrison in the head and he didn't want to play ever again. The first time we went fishing together, he hated the slimy scaliness of the fish.

From a very young age, Harrison displayed behaviors and characteristics that have stereotypically been associated with being gay. Feminine mannerisms and interests, as well as his desire to dress up, even in princess outfits, characterized Harrison's elementary years. Watching Harrison grow up proved to me that homosexuality is not a choice or a learned behavior. From his early years, Harrison was clearly on a path to the revelation that began around the campfire. While I cannot fully explain the science behind it, I can tell you that, as certain as I was when I was a young boy that Raquel Welch was hot, Harrison was just as certain at the same age that he liked Zac Efron.

After the campfire revelation, Harrison and I began a process of counseling through the Lutheran Counseling Center. We connected Harrison with a wonderful female counselor whose own father had been a pastor who eventually came out as being gay. This counselor was able to create the safe space needed for Harrison to openly discuss and wrestle with his feelings as he continued to move through puberty.

The topic of his sexuality was rarely, if ever, brought up with Harrison's mother. It was during these years that my relationship with Lisa was essential in helping me personally work through all the feelings and emotions that I was dealing with surrounding Harrison. Throughout this journey with Harrison, in addition to all the other pastoral and personal issues that I was handling, I was wrestling with my place in Harrison's story. I had my expectations as a father of what my first-born son would be. I had to dive into the theological and spiritual implications of this, not only as it pertained to my faith journey, but also the role I held as a pastor in a church body that openly condemned LGBTQ+ lifestyles as sinful. All this was impacted by the promise that I made to myself that I would never, ever, treat any of my children the way my father treated me. I was going to love them, no matter what, and they were always going to know it! I would not have been able to work through all of this and handle it as well as I did without the love and support of Lisa.

When the issues with my marriage came to a head, forcing my resignation from St. John's, that actually turned out to be a blessing for Harrison as he came to terms with his sexuality. My no longer being in the spotlight of ministering at the church provided Harrison the umbrella needed so that he could become comfortable enough to openly admit who he was as a gay person. Had I still been in the pulpit of St John's, I firmly believe that Harrison might have felt the need to continue to hide who he was out of the fear of what it might provoke in the church and my ministry.

It was in the spring of 2009, when Harrison was a junior, that he finally came to terms, once and for all, with his sexuality. We had just come back from his counseling session, and we were sitting outside our favorite pizza place in Sayville. Before we went in to pick up our pizza, Harrison said, "Dad, I have to tell you something ... I know that I am definitely gay." I sat there and I told him that I was glad that he was clear about this and that I loved him and would always love him and support him.

Not long after this revelation, a story would break in the New York news that would further my resolve in my role as his father. Tyler Clementi was a freshman at Rutgers University in the fall of 2010. His roommate secretly recorded Tyler kissing another man and used the footage to humiliate and bully Tyler for being gay. On September 22, 2010, Tyler jumped off the George Washington Bridge and killed himself. I swore in those moments when I heard that news that I was not going to lose my son because he was gay.

The next year or so would be an interesting journey for all of us. It would be another six months before Harrison would feel comfortable enough to share this with his mother and his siblings. Lisa and I believed that Samantha and Hunter would not be surprised by Harrison's revelation. We thought that they had suspected it all along. We were wrong about that. They were stunned and shocked but adjusted quickly, and we all laugh about it today. We got Harrison involved in a youth group that catered to the LGBTQ+ community and, in his zeal to show how proud he was in coming out, Harrison started a gay club at the high school during his senior year.

As Harrison moved on to college, he was finally able to put all of his favorite interests together. Throughout his life, Harrison loved to perform and put on shows. He loved to direct and develop his own stories. He especially loved dressing up and dancing. While in college, he discovered drag. Yup, folks, not only is my son gay, but he makes his living as a very good, very successful, drag performer.

I came to learn about Harrison's new love when I received a box at my home during the summer after his first year in college. Harrison's computer had been sent to Apple® for repair. A box the size of the computer came to my house and, thinking it was the computer and wanting to make sure that it arrived OK, I opened the box to check it. Well, it was not a computer. The box contained size 14, six-inch-high, red men's boots (think *Kinky Boots*). Upon making this discovery, I questioned Lisa with great angst, "Does he want to be a woman??? Can't he just be gay???" After some back-and-forth texts with Harrison, Lisa assured me that he didn't want to be a woman, but that he had found drag.

Today, Harrison performs under the stage name *Kimmi Moore*, an homage to his love for Britney Spears. Harrison designs all his costumes. He choreographs all his dances, which include backup dancers. He has recorded songs that he has written and made music videos that go along with them.

Needless to say, this certainly finalized the role that I had as a pastor prior to all of this. Before anything else, especially being a pastor, I was a father. Though I was in training to be a pastor when Harrison was born, he came first and, as I had promised myself, I was going to be that father that my dad was not. Therefore, any chance of my being a pastor again in the Lutheran Church-Missouri Synod was not a reality anymore. In the months following Harrison's revelation, I met with the bishop and shared all of this asking if he would release me into the process whereby I could leave my current Lutheran Church body and begin to transition into the Evangelical Lutheran Church in America. I will talk about these differences in a chapter toward the end of the book.

In order to make this transition, I had to wrestle with what the Bible says regarding homosexuality and how I would live with that spiritually, if I were ever to serve as a pastor again. While there are passages in the Bible that can be interpreted as condemning same-sex relationships, I believe that it is very important that we remember the purpose and central theme of the Bible before all the other historical, cultural, and societal matters it addresses. The central theme and purpose of the Bible is to reveal to us the hope, grace, and salvation that comes through Jesus Christ in the face of the sin and brokenness that we all deal with in the reality of life.

The Law, the Commandments, and the expectations that God gives in the Bible are to be followed to the best of our ability. The more we live our lives according to the instructions that God gives to us, the smoother and less painful, hopefully, our lives will be. The problem is that no one can keep the Law perfectly. No matter how hard we try, the sad reality of the sin we inherit at our birth is that we fall short of living perfect lives. Jesus came into the world, not to give us the perfect handbook on perfect living, but as the acknowledgment that sin is real and a regular part of our lives and that we need help, forgiveness, and hope in the face of sin.

I know that not all Christians will agree with me on this and that is OK. It's easy to hold a certain position in life until that position comes home to roost in one's own personal life. While the temptation exists to see everything as black and white, I have learned that practicing the Christian faith in real life is more often shades of grey. I have become comfortable with the church's acceptance of the LGBTQ+ community because I believe that issues of marriage and sexuality have evolved throughout history and even in the Bible.

There are many places in the Bible that are extremely troublesome when we approach them from our puritanical American picture of marriage, sexuality, and life. The growth and populating of creation after the Garden of Eden relies on our acceptance of blood relatives procreating with each other. Throughout the Bible and history, marriages were not built on love but were transactional, and women were often seen as property. Many of the main characters of the Bible had more than one wife. One of the passages that has always caused me to scratch my head was the story of David and Bathsheba.

In that story, King David, who has many wives and concubines, is out on his rooftop one day, and he looks and sees beautiful Bathsheba taking a bath. Upon seeing her beauty, David decides that he must have her. But Bathsheba is married to Uriah, a soldier in David's army. After David impregnates Bathsheba, he desperately wants to cover it up. He invites Uriah to a feast in the hopes that Uriah will become drunk and then go home and have sexual relations with his wife, covering up for David. But Uriah is so loyal to David that he instead goes and sleeps at the city gate to protect his king. Having no alternative, David sends Uriah to the front lines of the battle where he is killed. David murdered Uriah to cover his sin of adultery. Nathan the prophet is sent to call David out on his sin and to lead him to repentance. In calling him out Nathan says to David, *I gave you your master's house, and your master's wives into your bosom, and gave you the house of Israel and of Judah; and if that had been too little, I would have added as much more.* (2 Samuel 12:8 NRSV) Wait? What? More wives? More concubines? So the issue was not so much about sexuality but about coveting and taking what does not belong to you. And, on another note, keep in mind that the Bible tells us that Jesus was from the lineage of David, this broken, imperfect, sinner, who committed adultery and murder. More proof of how God works through broken, imperfect people for the work of the kingdom!

I don't want to dive too deeply into Bible study and theological debate. Instead, as the father of a gay son, and as a pastor who has been called to care for and minister to countless LGBTQ+ individuals and families throughout my entire ministry, I need to say that I do not believe God is expending a lot of thought and energy on these issues. There are much bigger issues for God to deal with. After all, if we are to accept that LGBTQ+ actions are sinful, we have to recognize that they didn't even make it into the top ten. None of the Ten Commandments address these issues. Lord knows, we all have our hands full just trying to keep and stay on top of those Ten Commandments without making these additional issues into mortal sins that lead to the express elevator to hell.

If we are to believe that God is love, which is indeed stated in the Bible, (see 1 John 4: 7-12), and we are to condemn as sinful and reject love between people of the same sex, then we may be getting in the way of carrying out the greatest commandment that Jesus gave to us when He said:

> *I give you a new commandment, that you love one another. Just as I have loved you, you also should love one another. By this everyone will know that you are my disciples, if you have love for one another.* (John 13: 34-35 NRSV)

I also don't want to spend time debating whether homosexuality is a sin or the product of a fallen creation or whether God made gay people that way. In my opinion, this is a fruitless effort. The reality of the world, as opposed to the fantasy that we often like to paint in our perfect pictures, is that the LGBTQ+ community is and always has been part of the world. They are part of God's creation. They are part of the world that God so loved when He sent His only Son to die on the cross. I have no doubt that the church is supposed to be a sanctuary and welcoming place for this community, just as the church welcomes everyone else, none of whom are perfect.

Of all of my children, Harrison has been the one I have had to work the hardest to connect with. My daughter, Samantha, has always been *Daddy's Little Girl* and the glue that has held together the rest of the family. My second son, Hunter, turned out to be that sports fanatic that I prayed for, so finding common interests was easy. But with Harrison, we had to work hard to communicate and understand each other. There were times when it was challenging and heartbreaking. But I thank God each day that God had such a wonderful sense of humor in answering my prayers the way that He did. Harrison has taught me the most about being a father–the father I wanted to be, not the father I had, or feared I would become. Harrison has made me a better, more loving, and accepting person. And because of that, Harrison made me a much better and more compassionate pastor.

This is why God sent His first-born son into the manger so long ago. God came to be near to us. All of us! So that we may know love.

Chapter 10
Divorce

Ms. E: Judge. Mr. Schenkel has one issue he would like to address with the Court.

Court: Sure.

Me: I have a question, Your Honor, because I don't know what to believe any more. It's created a lot of emotional difficulty and distress for me.

Court: You are no different than all the other litigants who go through this.

Me: It has to do with my former attorney, Ms. McG. After our April conference, when Ms. E. (ex-wife's attorney) had brought custody (of the children) into issue, Ms. McG reported to me that Ms. E. stated in court… something to the effect that my oldest son is gay and the father… wants nothing to do with him.

Court: I have to tell --- okay, what is your question?

Me: Well, when I no longer had Ms. McG as my attorney, I directly spoke to Ms. E. and asked her about that. She said, "Absolutely not, I would never, ever say something like that." She said she would talk to Ms. McG. She didn't have a chance to talk to Ms. McG, but one day, a little over a week ago, Ms. McG. caught Ms. E. in the hallway out there while I was on the phone. They got into a pretty nasty screaming match in the hall. Later on that evening Ms. E. had the courage to call and talk to me about it and again reiterated what she said.

Judge, I just wanted to know, from your point of view, was such a statement ever made, because it created a lot more anger and made it very difficult for cooperation in the course of the proceeding over the last several months.

Court: I first have to tell you, Mr. Schenkel, that I have over 300 cases on my docket and I don't necessarily remember every conference. However, I do take copious notes. There is nothing in my notes to indicate that such a statement was made and it's an unusual statement, so I think I might remember it, if it was made, and I don't recall anything of that nature.

Me: That's what I needed to know. Thank you.

Ms. E: If I may make one comment on the record that I have been wrongfully accused by a member of the Bar of making such a statement to a court about someone's child's sexual preference.

Divorce sucks! No matter the reason ... no matter the

circumstances … no matter who is at fault … no matter what was said … no matter who did what …. A divorce is far more work and is far more painful and more costly in terms of time, energy, and money than a wedding is. When you go through a divorce, you learn a lot. You learn a lot about the legal system. You learn who your friends and family are. You learn what you can stand up against. You learn what really matters in life. I learned many unexpected–and sometimes very painful lessons–as I went through divorce.

The first lesson that I learned is that the legal system does not care. It does not care why your marriage fell apart. It does not care about you as a human being. It does not care what it costs you or your family to get to a resolution. It does not make the situation any better or easier. Sadly, in both my personal divorce and in the many times during my ministry when I have cared for families going through a divorce, this has been the case. In my opinion, many of those who practice matrimonial law count on the system to exasperate the emotional firepower between the divorcing parties, in the hopes of more billable hours. As I write these words, I still find myself struggling to have respect for anyone who practices matrimonial law.

The exchange above is taken directly from the court transcript regarding my divorce on October 8, 2009. The background to that day in court started over a year earlier when the legal process of divorce began for me and Linda, my soon-to-be ex-wife. From the beginning, I wanted to use a process of mediation to work through the details of the divorce. We did not have many earthly possessions to fight over. We lived in church-owned housing, so there was no house to divide. What we had more than anything else was debt. From the beginning of the official divorce process, I was willing to take responsibility for the debt (which would push me to the brink of bankruptcy). We had already, on our own, worked out a visitation schedule for the children that shared them equally; and that schedule had been working for all parties involved. I was willing to pay whatever child support the New York state mathematical formula determined. It should have been a quick and easily resolved divorce.

However, the emotions involved in divorce can quickly overwhelm the rational mind. The party in the divorce who feels they were *wronged* more often wants blood or a pound of flesh. Friends and family members are all too willing to offer their own *expert* advice. They can be too emotionally attached to the situation to really offer productive, unbiased assistance.

Within a few months of officially filing for divorce, Linda and I had an agreement drawn up that outlined all the things that I had agreed to. But Linda, on the advice of her friends, fired her attorney and decided she wanted to battle this out in court.

I retained the attorney from Sayville who had helped me in the situation with my parents, the attorney to whom I also had referred several parishioners over the years. Ms. McG. turned out, as seen in the above transcript, to be no friend of mine or my family. I deeply regret that I entrusted to her care several beloved parishioners during my time at St. John's.

As the months went on, and Linda kept having her lawyer write useless letters over ridiculous issues, compounding the billable hours, I finally released my attorney and represented myself. I already had the written agreement that was previously drawn up. Because I wasn't trying to hide or deny anything, I felt confident that common sense would eventually prevail.

When you represent yourself (which I am in no way endorsing here), you have the opportunity to talk directly to the other party's lawyer and to the judge in the divorce case. I strongly encourage everyone going through a divorce to try a reputable legal mediation process before loading up on lawyers ready to carry your battle all the way to trial.

Had I not represented myself, I would have never known the truth regarding how my lawyer was despicably using emotional manipulation to further raise the tension level, along with the stakes, when it came to dissolving my marriage. The sad circumstances surrounding every divorce are bad enough as it is. They do not need to be further complicated by a legal system that should be advocating for those involved in a way that is helpful, not hurtful.

The episode regarding my son's sexuality helped to refocus our perspectives in a way that would enable us to more constructively move forward and eventually finalize our divorce. The settled agreement was far less than the original agreement that we worked out. Due to some unfortunate circumstances of poor judgment on the part of Linda, the court took away items that I had originally agreed to. As a result, the entire process would take almost three years before the divorce was finalized.

The lessons received from family, friends, and people I served at the church further compounded the emotions of going through divorce. The reality of the circumstances leading to my divorce were bad enough because they were factual, without the incessant need of so many who would gossip and offer their own perspectives. This I somewhat expected, because I was a public figure but not to the extent to which it was carried. When the process first began, the temptation existed to fight back and try to set the record straight. But after a little while, I learned that it doesn't really matter. People are going to talk, no matter what. Therefore, it is important to approach divorce with integrity, to do the right thing, so you can look in the mirror and, if children are involved, be able to honestly look them in the eye and answer their questions as they move forward in life in a way that you can be proud of yourself and how you handled things. In time, I developed a sense of humor about it all and often joked that it would be fun to sit back with a bucket of popcorn and learn about what happened next.

What was unexpected, and what I was unprepared for, was the reaction I would receive from some of the people with whom I had walked through some of the darkest and most painful moments of their lives. Some of the people who turned against me and were the most harsh and vile in their reaction to my divorce and to my leaving my ministry at the church were the people who, if I ever broke the seal of confession and told the story of the things I dealt with as their pastor, would be greatly embarrassed and humiliated. It was a lesson in healthy boundaries for later on in life and ministry.

The most unexpected of all relationship reactions to my divorce was from my sister. Admittedly, she was in a very hard place, being married to the brother of my soon-to-be ex-wife. The closeness that we all shared was shattered along with our marriage. I knew that in changing my life it would change the manner in which I had a relationship with my sister. But I never expected that it would put an end to our relationship permanently. My sister cut me off from my two nieces and made covert attempts to "protect" my own children from me. My sister would also cut my Aunt Carolee and Uncle Bill out of her own life because they continued to have a relationship with me. Before he died, my Uncle Bill desperately tried to reconcile with my sister and open the door to a future relationship between my sister and me. But she coldly rejected his attempts and basically wished him a good death.

The lesson I learned as a pastor going through divorce

reinforced my conviction that the church must always be a sanctuary! The church has to be a safe and welcoming place for people who are going through pain, upheaval, and trauma, even in divorce.

Throughout her history, the church has wrestled with how to handle parishioners who get divorced. There are still Christian denominations that exclude divorced people from receiving the Sacrament of Holy Communion. Up until recent history, the divorce of a pastor would automatically eliminate the pastor from ever performing pastoral duties again.

It is important that the Christian church take marriage and divorce very seriously. Jesus's words regarding marriage and divorce are clear. Jesus repeatedly upheld the importance and sanctity of marriage. The Scriptures refer to Jesus's love for us, His Church, as the love of a groom for his bride. He showed the depth of that love by giving His life for His bride the church, and Jesus continues to hold this out as the standard for marriage. In speaking about the reality of divorce, Jesus condemns it in the strongest possible terms. Therefore, it is of the highest duties and obligations for the Christian to approach marriage in the most serious of ways. Divorce should not be taken lightly or as a matter of convenience. After all, God's laws and expectations for our lives are good, pure, and to be aspired to.

But Jesus did not come into the world because things always go right and life is lived perfectly. Divorce is the result of the brokenness that plagues the world on a daily basis. Sin brings brokenness. Divorce is brokenness. When a marital relationship is broken so badly by the sins and imperfections of the world, no amount of law and commandments can fix it or bring comfort to the situation.

Therefore, the church must be a place of grace and healing. People who have failed at their marriage do not need to be reminded of it, nor do they need the emotional fallout from the marriage to be further complicated by the church's rejection of them. Now, more than ever, people who are divorced need the church, and the main mission of the church, which is to bring healing and new life through the work and the presence of Jesus.

Chapter 11
In All These Things...

My cell phone rang, waking me up around 5:30 a.m. on Wednesday, May 27, 2009. It was Lisa calling from the first-floor apartment where she and her daughter Mackenzie were now living. "Harry," she said in a quiet whisper, "The FBI is here. They have guns and bulletproof vests on. They just broke down the front door upstairs." "You have got to be kidding!" But she was not. She was crouching down, hiding next to a window where she could see outside, and she said, "They are here arresting the landlord upstairs." "I am on my way," I responded. I quickly threw on my clothes and drove the ten minutes from my apartment to hers.

By the time I arrived, the excitement was just about over. The final unmarked cars were pulling away with Lisa's landlord handcuffed in the backseat. Lisa had come outside, and we were able to question the remaining FBI agents to determine if it was unsafe to live in the house anymore. They informed us that the landlord, who had been working as a banker, was being arrested, along with several other financiers in the New York City area, for running a Ponzi-type mortgage fraud scheme, totaling more than ten million dollars in ill-gotten gains.

For weeks before the FBI raid, Lisa had been telling me that she felt like she was being watched and followed. I would dismiss her concerns, saying that our personal situation was not something that was worthy of private investigators and the drama that they bring. To my shock on that early spring morning, she turned out to be right. Although she was not being watched and followed for her own reasons, she was being watched and followed because the FBI was assessing whether or not she was connected to her landlord in any other way than renting his first-floor apartment.

That's what the stress and anxiety of divorce does to you. In the midst of all the mudslinging and accusations, worry and paranoia set in and cause you to start seeing things around every corner. No decision made in the midst of a divorce is a simple, easy decision. Every decision is analyzed as to how it may affect the legal proceedings or what impact it has on one's personal future, as well as how it affects the rest of the family. It was no delusional stretch of thought to think that we were being followed and investigated in the midst of our divorce proceedings. Even though we were being followed by the FBI, fortunately, it had nothing to do with us!

The time following my official resignation as the pastor of St. John's, Sayville, was an interesting and stress-filled time, to say the least, with its share of weird moments like the FBI raid. While I was dealing with going to court, processing Harrison's revelation, and acclimating and adjusting to the changing direction and dynamics of family with visitation and co-parenting, I also needed to figure out my career. Yet, as God promises in Romans 8:28, God is at work in all things for His good and purpose.

I had moved into a one-bedroom basement apartment in Glen's house. Glen is the parishioner I described in Chapter 7; he was run over by his wife's ex-husband. The arrangement was a mutually beneficial blessing. I was able to find an affordable place in the area near the children's school and activities, and I was able to help Glen around the house with some of the duties that were no longer easy for him to perform.

I would vacuum and winterize the pool, clean up the fall leaves, and do other small things that we all too often take for granted.

Within two months of resigning from the church, while I was still helping my friend with carpentry, I was hired by Thrivent Financial as a financial associate. Thrivent Financial is a Fortune 500 financial services organization. It began in 1902 as a partner to the ministry of the Lutheran Church. The predecessor bodies of Thrivent helped assist church members with their finances as well as their need for protection through insurance products.

As a fraternal company, Thrivent Financial is membership-based and tied to a clearly defined mission. That mission is to make smart financial decisions and choices guided by Christian values. Thrivent works in direct partnership with the Lutheran Church. Educational seminars are held at churches to introduce people of faith to the different options that exist for their financial health and well-being. The fraternal aspect of the organization includes tax advantages that allow Thrivent to redirect funds back toward churches and ministry partners and such global organizations as Habitat for Humanity.

For me personally, being hired by Thrivent Financial was another one of God's little gifts to put me where I needed to be at the right time. Throughout my pastoral ministry, I always had a desire to learn and know more about financial matters but never really had the time to pursue it. I listened to the Wall Street update on the radio each day and wondered what the ups and downs of the market really meant – things like short selling, hedge funds, asset classes, and mutual funds, just to name a few. I made decisions regarding church finances and the budget on a regular basis but never fully understood all the different factors surrounding money and the things that can be done with it. The first several months of 2009 immersed me in the world of finances while keeping me connected to the church. Not only did I get to learn about all the ins and outs of money as I studied to pass the Series 7 and 66 licensing requirements, but I also remained directly connected to the mission and culture of the church, as I served and visited churches in the metro New York area on behalf of Thrivent. What I learned at that time regarding finances has come to be a great blessing in my current work as a pastor.

From 2009 until early 2013 I did this work for Thrivent primarily in Queens, Brooklyn, and Manhattan. I was blessed to visit dozens of different churches to share the benefits that Thrivent offered while seeing God at work in so many different ways in the multicultural microcosm of the world that is New York City. The schedule that Thrivent offered to me during this time was absolutely crucial in finding the healing that my family and I needed as we began rebuilding our lives. At Thrivent, I was able to control my schedule more than when I served as a pastor. This allowed me the time I needed to go to counseling, deal with court matters, and be available for my children as they navigated this new direction in life. It was also during this time that I was able to go through the official steps necessary to change my affiliation from the Lutheran Church-Missouri Synod (LCMS) to the Evangelical Lutheran Church in America (ELCA).

While I was finding a new direction at Thrivent, Lisa was also finding a new direction for her career. She started working for AHRC Suffolk. At the time she was hired, AHRC stood for the Association Helping Retarded Children. Since then, it has become known by the more politically correct name of the Association for Habitation and Residential Care. AHRC Suffolk was founded with the desire to help and serve children and adults with intellectual and other disabilities.

In the aftermath of the FBI raid, Lisa quickly determined that she could not live in the house of an alleged criminal while she was in the midst of her own divorce. For a short period of time, she found an apartment near Mackenzie's school. She hated that apartment. This inspired the next move that would impact all our lives in the most beautiful of ways.

In early 2010, Lisa was offered the position of houseparent at the Oakdale AHRC home where she had been working. As houseparent, Lisa would become the primary manager and caretaker of nine mentally disabled adults who lived in that home. They ranged in age from the late thirties into their eighties. As the houseparent, Lisa was responsible for everything from their medications to their finances to where they would go together as a group on vacation each summer. Part of the job responsibility was that Lisa, and subsequently her family, would live in a small one-bedroom apartment connected to the house. This was another answer to prayer.

The apartment was perfect for Lisa and Mackenzie (and eventually me) to live in. What we did not expect was, after we were married in early 2012, that all our children would live there with us more and more of the time. To accommodate the children, we modified the apartment in a way that the producers of the *Transformers®* movies would envy. The apartment kitchen doubled as the master bedroom. We had a Murphy Bed that came down out of a cabinet that was attached to the kitchen table (which also doubled as the desk for homework and other projects). The closet in the living room had another Murphy Bed that came out of it for Hunter when he slept over. The one bedroom in the apartment housed a bunk bed for Samantha and Mackenzie. By this time, Harrison had gone off to college and did not need a permanent space.

It was during the time we lived in the group home that we purchased a camper. The camper would serve as our refuge and escape on weekends from April through October. To truly recharge, Lisa needed to leave the house on weekends, while a weekend relief houseparent took over. We spent many wonderful weekends overlooking the Atlantic Ocean or the Peconic Bay or the wooded treescape of the Long Island Pine Barrens.

Aside from all the economic benefits received from Lisa's job at AHRC came an appreciation for people and life that I don't think our children could have ever learned anywhere else. Living with the residents of AHRC helped to reinforce for all of us what really matters in life. It helped put things into perspective. It gave us an appreciation for the little things and gifts of life. You could never really tell the age of the residents of the Oakdale AHRC house. Why? Because they never stressed about anything! If they got into a fight or got mad at each other, they would call it out quickly, and then it would be over, just as quickly as it began.

When Lisa first moved in, the oldest member of the house was Ruth, who was blind and in her eighties. Ruth would sit all day and listen to books on tape. She was diagnosed with serious, stage four breast cancer and was expected to only live for a few months. But she didn't know that she was supposed to stress and think about that! She lived for another two years with that cancer. It got so bad that it started to break through her skin, but that didn't faze her. Throughout her final months, Ruth would continue to smile and laugh and brighten the lives of the people around her.

If Lisa's job at AHRC had been only about dealing with and caring for the residents, we could have maybe lived there for the rest of our lives. But unfortunately, AHRC was government-funded and regulated, meaning that the original mission and intent upon which AHRC was founded were constantly being redefined and manipulated by government officials who rarely, if ever, had any experience with the population. Unfortunately, no longer able to deal with the administrative nonsense and incompetence, Lisa resigned from the position in October 2017. But those nearly ten years of service at AHRC were another one of God's gifts that got us to the place we needed to go.

About a year after resigning from St. John's, my career at Thrivent brought me into contact with an ELCA church and pastor in Jamaica, Queens, who was looking for a little help with his ministry. He was not looking for anything extensive, just a part-time assistant who could preach every once in a while and take on a few special projects. I was greatly enjoying all the new experiences that I was having at Thrivent, but I missed preaching and being in the church as a pastor. His offer was just what I needed. I could do a little bit of the pastor thing while still focusing most of my energy on my family and my obligations to Thrivent.

For the next two and a half years, while working at Thrivent, I served part-time at Our Saviour Lutheran Church in Jamaica, Queens. I would take the train from Ronkonkoma to Jamaica Station every Sunday and then take a cab to the church. Lisa would drive in later in the morning and we would drive home together. The church was a multiethnic foretaste of what heaven should look like. There were people of all colors and backgrounds, all gathered around God's gifts of Word and Sacrament. In my time there, I started to feel God leading me back deeper into pastoral ministry.

In late 2011, I became aware that Transfiguration Lutheran Church in Harlem, New York, was looking for a part-time pastor. The church was located right around the corner from the world-famous soul food restaurant, Sylvia's. The church was primarily an African-American church right in the heart of Harlem and a ten-minute walk from the Apollo Theater.

As a child who came of age in the 1980s, I had come to the notion that race was no longer a major issue. During my teenage years, most of our favorite celebrities and influential personalities were people of color. Michael Jackson, Eddie Murphy, Whitney Houston, and Prince ruled the airwaves and were imitated at every opportunity. Oprah Winfrey was our virtual after-school advisor. This is not to mention all of the sports stars that we emulated and idolized. And, for me personally, the majority of my friends at my high school were people of color. When Transfiguration came on my radar, Barack Obama, was the president of the United States.

Having this as my background and life experience, I didn't think twice about the opportunity to serve as a white pastor in Harlem. I left my service in Jamaica and joyfully began serving in Harlem with the hopes of reinvigorating the ministry of Transfiguration so that they could continue to serve the people of Harlem. We were so excited about this new opportunity with all its possibilities that Lisa and I decided one of the first things we would do at Transfiguration was get married there. So, the day after New Year's Day, still technically part of the Christmas season, we were married and had a small family reception around the corner at Sylvia's.

I accepted the call to Transfiguration. In my six months of serving as their part-time pastor, I learned how wrong I was. Half of the members of the church were unhappy that they were being served by a white male pastor. No matter what I suggested or tried to accomplish at this fledgling church, I was met with opposition and resistance.

The saddest part of all this was that my children loved

this church. They were dazzled by the lively, soulful music that wrapped itself around the traditional, historic liturgy of the church. But as my tenure there came to an end in a heated congregational meeting right before Father's Day 2012, the children saw how deep the scars of racism can run and how even the best of intentions regarding God's work can be derailed. Just three years later, the church would close its doors.

This short tenure and negative experience was a gut punch to my confidence. It caused me to question whether I still had it in me to continue to be a pastor. I was deeply concerned that, because I was new to the Evangelical Lutheran Church in America, the way my time in Harlem transpired would call into question my pastoral leadership and ability, especially in the aftermath of my divorce. For the next several months I would wallow around in pastoral purgatory. I had no church to serve consistently. That Christmas was painful. Just when I thought that everything was coming back together, I had nowhere to go and no church to serve in, during my favorite time of the year.

Sometimes amid the chaos and struggle brought by sin, it's easy to forget that God is still in charge and that God has a plan, even when we don't. A few weeks after my time in Harlem ended, a pastor friend called asking a favor. He was scheduled to preach for a couple of Sundays at a church in East Northport that had recently lost their pastor. My friend lived in the city and did not have a car. After he accepted the invitation to cover the church, he realized how much trouble it was going to be to get there. Knowing that I was free and lived less than a half hour from the church, he asked me to take the assignment. Still stinging and hurting, yet welcoming the chance for some additional income, I grudgingly accepted the invitation.

That Sunday in late July 2012 at St. Paul's Lutheran Church, East Northport would change the course of our lives for the next eight years (and beyond) and show me once again how God is in charge and how His church, despite all that can go wrong in the world and even in the church, is still a sanctuary.

Chapter 12
From Long Island to Longwood

Coincidence (*noun*)
1. A remarkable concurrence of events or circumstances without an apparent causal connection
2. A correspondence in the nature of or in the time of occurrence.

During over fifty years of life and faith, I have come to no longer believe in coincidences. In my privilege of serving as a pastor, many things that could be chalked up to coincidence, fate, or luck have been the right gift in the right place at the right time. Everything happens for a reason. Sometimes it's a good reason. Sometimes it's a bad reason. (But I firmly believe that there is something bigger, greater, and beyond ourselves, and any sense of understanding on our part, that is working in our lives.) We just need to be aware of it. Sometimes I like to call it *divine coincidence*. It's those things that happen in our lives that cause us to look up over our shoulder to see if God (or whatever deity we call upon in our lives) is standing there over us.

When Lisa and I stepped into St. Paul's Lutheran Church, East Northport on Sunday, July 29, 2012, there was a buzz in the lobby of the church. This was the second straight Sunday I was preaching there after the invitation from my friend who did not want to make the trip from New York City.

The prior Sunday was eye-opening for all of us. I was

shocked to learn St. Paul's was coming to the end of their interim ministry and would soon be searching for a new pastor. An interim ministry time is when a church has a pastor come in, who will not be their permanent pastor, to help the church move through some issues, emotions, and challenges that may have resulted from the prior pastor's tenure. St. Paul's needed an intentional interim ministry because their prior pastors, a husband-and-wife team, had left the church in a state of division over issues regarding their leadership as well as the role of the parochial school that was part of the church campus.

So after more than two years of the interim pastor helping to clean up the church's finances and begin the process of emotional healing and rebuilding, the time had come for St. Paul's to begin the search for a new permanent pastor. They had just formed their call committee–the group of members of the church, from all ages and interests in the church, who would help to consider who should become their next pastor.

Upon our return for my second week of coverage, while the interim pastor was on vacation, some members of the call committee met us in the lobby because they wanted to ask me some questions about my ministry and availability. I was somewhat embarrassed to have to answer that I was not serving in a church because of the difficulties in Harlem. Yet that didn't seem to deter them in any way. In particular, they were interested in the fact that I had graduated from Long Island Lutheran High School (LuHi).

I learned that much of the tension that existed leading to the end of the tenure of the prior pastors was that St. Paul's Lutheran School, a preschool through fifth grade, had now become Long Island Lutheran Day School (LuDay), a part of LuHi. There was much turbulence that existed as a result of this restructuring. When the economy took a downturn in 2008, St. Paul's Lutheran School incurred enormous debt in an effort to continue to survive. For nearly forty years, the school had enjoyed a fine reputation and a full enrollment. But then some of the struggles with the pastors of the church spilled over to the school and, when the economy soured, enrollment suffered.

For years, many St. Paul's Lutheran School students who graduated from fifth grade would go on to sixth grade at LuHi. St. Paul's School was a natural feeder school for the middle school and high school at LuHi. At the same time, as part of its long-range planning, LuHi had been seriously considering expanding to include the elementary academic years, but they had no room on the Brookville campus to do this.

When St. Paul's Lutheran School ran into trouble, they took the courageous step of approaching LuHi about taking over the school instead of having to make the heart-wrenching decision to close the school. In 2010, LuHi took control of St. Paul's School. In a formal sense, as an incorporated institution, St. Paul's Lutheran School did close. However, the majority of the staff and teachers were hired by LuDay, and most of the students who had been enrolled in St Paul's School subsequently reenrolled in LuDay.

When I arrived at St. Paul's, I quickly learned that there were many conflicting emotions among both the church members and the staff at the school regarding the fact that the school was no longer St. Paul's but now LuDay. Church members were still mourning the loss and apparent failure of their beloved school. LuDay staff, who had formerly been employed at St. Paul's School, were lamenting the changes and the more intentional business structure that LuHi had instituted into the newly formed LuDay.

As a Lutheran Pastor who had graduated from LuHi and credited my time at LuHi as one of the main reasons why I was led into Holy Ministry, the call committee could immediately see that I might be God's tool to help calm the waters between

St. Paul's and LuDay and to lead them into the future.

On that second Sunday I filled in at St. Paul's, I preached a thought-provoking sermon asking the question about whether we could meet James Holmes in heaven. On Friday, July 20, just nine days earlier, Holmes had entered a movie theater in Aurora, Colorado, during the screening of the Batman movie *The Dark Knight Rises,* and had opened fire, killing twelve people and injuring seventy others. In preaching about the power of God's grace, I posed the question of whether God's grace could cover this heinous sin should the assailant come to faithful repentance. The point of the sermon was to remind everyone that, ultimately, God is the judge of all things, not us. And that we might be surprised by who we meet in heaven.

I would find out after I was called to be the next pastor at St. Paul's on March 17, 2013, that that sermon played an integral role in leading the call committee to seriously consider me as their next pastor. The sermon, combined with my being a LuHi alum, sealed the deal and set us off together as pastor and people for several years of joyful ministry together. This surely was a blessed divine coincidence.

I was renewed and reinvigorated by the call to St. Paul's. It was a genuine healing experience in many ways. The damage to my confidence after the implosion in Harlem was overcome. It was reassuring to know that a church still saw value in my pastoral abilities. More importantly, the fallout from my divorce was finally coming to a close. St. Paul's embraced us as the new blended family that we were. I also resigned from my position at Thrivent Financial. The call at St. Paul's was a full-time call meaning that I would no longer have any time to work at Thrivent. This was another gift of God's good timing. Even after the struggles in Harlem, I still found myself being pulled back to full-time pastoral ministry. That was one of the reasons why the way my time in Harlem ended hurt so badly. I was feeling called back to full-time ministry but wasn't sure if I could do it anymore or if anyone would want me anymore. The more I felt called back to the church full-time, the less my heart was in the work I was doing at Thrivent. God saw that and, in God's immutable ways, God took care of it.

My ministry at St. Paul's was joyful and energizing. I relished the privilege of serving as the pastor at a church with a school on campus. Even though LuDay was no longer the church's school, as the pastor of St. Paul's, I was the LuDay campus pastor. I led chapel with the students each Wednesday. I walked the halls and ministered to the children, their families, and the school staff. I sat on the school board as an ex-officio member able to have a say in school issues and how they affected the church. This was a dream of mine. Because LuHi meant so much to me and my journey to the ministry, I always dreamed of having a church with an elementary or high school attached to it. By God's grace, I was able to use my role as the pastor who was also a product of LuHi to bridge the gap in trust and to cultivate a more cooperative environment between the church and the school.

Lisa and I were also partnered now, not only in life but also in ministry. Within months of our coming to St. Paul's, LuDay was in need a of new art teacher. Throughout her life, Lisa had been an artist painting beautiful wall murals, house portraits, and other pictures as her heart was moved. She has always dreamed of teaching. When the LuDay art teacher quit the day before the new school year started, Lisa jumped at the opportunity. She thrived in the environment because it was fueled by her love for art and her love for children. She was able to balance teaching art two days a week to children from kindergarten to fifth grade while continuing her job as the houseparent for the AHRC home in Oakdale. It was joyful for me to be sharing many days and activities with her as we sought to serve and love the people of St. Paul's and LuDay.

All of this was humming along beautifully until the fall of 2017. A perfect storm of events in a short period of time threw everything into chaos. Over the course of just a few months, several different unconnected circumstances caused LuDay to unravel. The Northport school district finally, after years of consideration, decided to offer full-day kindergarten in the public school system. Immediately, fall enrollment for kindergarten at LuDay was cut by over two-thirds. The kindergarten was the largest class at LuDay and supplemented the income for most of the other classes. At the same time, enrollment at LuHi had fallen by over a hundred students in one year. This was a loss of over a million dollars in enrollment income. Now margins were much smaller and there was no room for deficit spending. At the same time, the head of school at LuHi and LuDay was embroiled in a marital scandal that sucked up the remaining focus and energy of the leadership.

In the fall of 2017, we were informed by LuHi leadership that LuDay was on the ropes and that we needed to up the ante when it came to enrollment. Unfortunately, it was already too late. Circumstances were too overwhelming by that point. A few months later, in January 2018, the decision was made that LuDay would not continue past June.

Just like that, the primary reason and purpose of why I was called to be the pastor at St. Paul's was turned upside down. By the summer of 2018, the school was gone, and now I had to figure out what St. Paul's was going to do with the school building, playground, and property while also figuring out what my place was as the pastor of St. Paul's.

I spent the following year putting the word out to the community that we were open to partnering in new directions for ministry and service to the community. I met with several people and groups who had some interesting proposals for the building and property. A group of LuDay parents tried to get momentum behind continuing the school as St. Paul's Academy, but the finances didn't make sense. Ministries to addiction rehab and youth outreach were also considered, but the investment needed to get these efforts off the ground was too much to ask in a short period of time.

The last thing I wanted to consider for the building and property was another school. In the last ten years, the people of St. Paul's had gone through the emotional upheaval of closing two different school entities. It was my hope that we could utilize the assets of the church in a different way other than a school. But as usual, God has a sense of humor and loves to take us in directions that we don't want to go. Usually, this is to remind us of who is still in charge, especially in the midst of chaos.

I came back to my office one afternoon after making hospital visits and my office manager gave me a message to call John Tunney and Mimosa Jones. They wanted to talk to me about using the building for a new school. I immediately dismissed this, telling the office manager I did not want to talk to them because I was not interested in a school. My office manager insisted, telling me, "You need to listen to them; they have a unique idea that might just work." So, at her insistence, I set up the appointment.

By the end of my hour-long meeting with John and Mimosa, not only was I sold on the idea, but I also became their number one salesman. John was a very successful restaurateur and an entrepreneur. Mimosa formerly was a Hollywood screenwriter and occasional contributor to Fox News regarding education. During her time as a screenwriter, Mimosa deeply studied education, especially the work of Maria Montessori. From her studies, she wrote a screenplay about the life of

Montessori. Mimosa also came to realize that many of the educational principles that guided Montessori's work, and the schools named after her, had been largely forgotten. Mimosa also studied *Reggio Emilia* educational philosophy. From her research, John and Mimosa developed the idea for "The School House." This would be a new approach to education that centered on the needs of the child through what they were calling the *American Emergent Curriculum.*

Classrooms at The School House would not be set up with desks in rows. This was a relic, not of education, but of janitors' unions, who found that it was easier to clean classrooms with desks in a row. Pictures and water stations in the school would be hung low, at a child's level. Classrooms would look nothing like typical classrooms. Carpets, seating areas, and group tables would be found at all levels. The disciplines of math, science, reading, and other skills are not separate subjects but intertwined into projects that build life skills. For example, in the first year of The School House, the children designed, built, and marketed their own farm stand. One level of children did the math needed to design the farm stand. Another level of children planted vegetables and cared for egg-producing chickens on campus. Another level of children wrote an advertisement and then reached out to a local news channel for an interview and exposure of the farm stand. Every Thursday the farm stand would open with students and parents running it, bringing in hundreds of dollars for the students' activities.

One year after the close of LuDay, The School House was renovating the building, and in the fall of 2019, it opened its doors. So hungry was the community for a new approach to education that enrollment was full for the first year, and each subsequent year has had a lengthy waiting list. The success of The School House was a welcome gift and blessing for St. Paul's after the heartbreak of schools past.

While the nature of my ministry at St. Paul's was called into question in the aftermath of the closure of LuDay, I also found that my attitude regarding New York and my continued ministry there were also coming into question. This was the culmination of many years of frustration as a born-and-bred New Yorker. The ongoing hostility that comes with living in the metro New York area was wearing on me after all those years. Everything in New York is a competition–from driving to being in line at a store, to the one-upmanship of who's got the latest and greatest of whatever is new. Additionally, throughout my ministry of nearly twenty-five years, I was growing tired of the increasing hostility aimed at the Church and her ministry. When I first started as a pastor in New York, whenever I wore my clergy collar, people would often stop me and ask for a prayer or for me to bless something, or for me to go visit someone in the hospital and share a word of encouragement. In the aftermath of the clergy sex scandals, encounters like that became less and less frequent. Also, participation in church was rapidly decreasing. All the other demands of life, and making children *well-rounded* with soccer practice, music lessons, tutoring, and all the other activities, made church just another choice among many programs. The economic realities of New York were also making it increasingly difficult for younger couples, who would soon welcome children, to come into communities and buy the homes of older people who were moving on. The median age of many towns on Long Island was getting older and older, meaning fewer and fewer children.

In January 2020, I turned fifty years old and was on the verge of celebrating my twenty-fifth year as a pastor. Moments like that invite a great deal of reflection. I had come through many things during my life and ministry. After the close of

LuDay and then being able to repurpose the building in a way that benefited the community and St. Paul's, I was starting to feel like my ministry at St. Paul's was coming to a close. Couple that with my increasing annoyance at living in New York, and I was beginning to think about a change.

One day during that birthday month, while Lisa and I were sitting in our hot tub at the house we had recently purchased in Pennsylvania, I said to her, "I'm starting to think that I will no longer finish my ministry in New York and then retire. I am thinking that I may need to make one more move to another church, maybe outside New York." This hit Lisa like a brick. Her mom, her family, and her whole life had been in New York, mostly the Sayville area. For her to consider a move, especially out of state, would require an act of God. Well, that's what divine coincidences are for.

That conversation in the hot tub was intended to be one of those thinking-out-loud hypothetical what-if discussions that couples often engage in that turn into nothing. One week after that private conversation, I received a weird email. In the subject line in all caps, it read: "CONFIDENTIAL, FOR YOUR EYES ONLY–PASTOR." I was about to delete it unopened, thinking that it was some spam email notifying me that I had won eleven million dollars from Nigeria when I realized that it said "pastor." So, I opened it. It was from a pastor who was retiring, after twenty-five years, from a church in Florida. He got my name from someone I went to LuHi with over thirty years earlier. He wanted to know if I would consider having a conversation about succeeding him at the church in Florida.

Holy S*%t! Evidently, Lisa and I were not alone in the hot tub a week earlier. I sat back in my office chair, looked over my shoulder to see if God was literally standing there with a grin on His face, and thought about how I was going to show this to Lisa. It became immediately clear to me that something was happening, and we needed to get ready for it.

I raced home and shared the email with Lisa. After a few minutes, while I watched the color drain and then subsequently return to her face, she said, "You can have a discussion with him, but that's it; don't make any promises or anything." After a couple of discussions with the pastor, it became clear that this was not a good fit for me, but it seriously opened the door for Lisa and me to talk about what it might look like if we left Long Island and where we would consider moving to. These discussions would kick into overdrive just two months later when New York, along with the rest of the world, shut down because of COVID-19.

Within the first three months of COVID-19 shutting down St. Paul's and all of New York, I knew that my time at St. Paul's and in New York was coming to an end. The way New York handled COVID-19 flattened the church and the ministries we had worked so hard to build, and I knew that I didn't have it in my heart to be the pastor who would rebuild it all when the pandemic was over. I had major problems with the inconsistencies in governance and the decisions that were made. I was most upset about the fact that liquor stores were considered essential businesses and were allowed to remain open, while I had to close the church's Alcoholics-Anonymous group, which welcomed over one hundred members each week. By the end of the first summer of COVID-19, the AA group had lost contact with over two-thirds of the members who attended. Great idea, New York. Leave the liquor stores open while cutting off the lifeline to those who struggled with it, at a time when they needed the support the most.

There were many more examples like this that just made it clear to me that my life would be healthier living somewhere else. In May 2020, because we were pre-recording video church services, Lisa came up with the idea of our driving to Florida to visit Samantha to see what it might be like if we lived in Florida. Samantha moved to Florida three days after she graduated from college in May 2017 to be near her boyfriend, who is now her husband. We drove to Florida, having to check in at the border, and spent two weeks roaming around Florida and talking about what ministry and life might look like there.

On the last Sunday of the year, I would announce to the beloved people of St. Paul's that God had called me to be the pastor of St. Stephen Lutheran Church, Longwood, Florida, a community in the Orlando area.

I am really starting to love those *divine coincidences.*

Chapter 13
We're Going to Disney World

God has a fantastic sense of humor, especially when God has a plan for your life. Yet we still often want to resist, bargain, and negotiate with God.

As we continued to deal with the effects of COVID-19 in the latter half of 2020, it became more and more apparent to both me and Lisa that we needed a change in our lives, both personally and professionally. For Lisa, however, the idea of leaving New York was deeply emotional and challenging. Lisa's entire life had been spent in the Sayville area. Unlike me, she had not only her mother but also several family members who lived nearby on Long Island. While being open to God's direction and the possibility of a move, Lisa decided that she was going to put some parameters and conditions on where we could move in the hopes that maybe it wouldn't happen.

Thinking that she could negotiate with God, Lisa decided that she would only consider a move from Long Island to Florida if it was to the Orlando area. Her mother wintered as a *snowbird* a few miles from Disney World. Samantha, our first child to be engaged and possibly the first to bring forth grandchildren, lived in Orlando. And finally, Lisa had a lifelong dream of working at Walt Disney World. Throughout her life, since 1973, Lisa and her family made their family vacation trips to Disney World. Many of her happiest childhood and family memories were made at "The Most Magical Place On Earth" (as the sign says that welcomes everyone onto Disney World property). So beloved is Disney World to her family that when

Lisa's parents retired, they became seasonal workers at Disney World. To all of these conditions, God seemingly said, "Challenge accepted."

On the day after election day 2020, I received an email from the bishop's office in Florida, asking to arrange a time for a Zoom "getting-to-know-you" meeting in the days following. Two days later the virtual meeting with the bishop's assistant transpired. Twenty minutes into the getting-to-know-you session, the conversation took an unexpected turn. "Ok, you are exactly who your bishop in New York told us you were. Here's the real reason we wanted to talk to you. There's a church in Longwood that just asked their pastor to leave. They are in serious need of someone to come in quickly and help them work through many issues and challenges. We wanted to know if you would consider this?" Intrigued, I quickly pulled out my phone, hiding it from the Zoom camera, as I tried to find where in Florida this Longwood place was. There was no hiding my face when I learned that Longwood was a northeastern suburb of Orlando, a thirty-minute drive from Walt Disney World.

Yet again, another Holy S*%t moment of divine coincidence. This time, I couldn't even wait to get home to talk to Lisa. As soon as the Zoom meeting ended, I called her and in rapid-fire bullet sentences ran down the details. She was excited, stunned, anxious, and humbled all in a matter of moments. She also knew that God had won. On January 21, 2021, we left New York.

God had been at work in another amazing way preparing us for this moment. Having lived in church housing throughout my entire ministry and then subsequently going through the divorce, I had never owned a home and had very little financial security. During Christmas 2018, Lisa's family rented a home in Pennsylvania to gather everyone together to celebrate the holidays. While we visited with them, we learned how affordable homes were in the area, and that began conversations about the possibility of Lisa and me buying a home as an investment and future living space. A few months later in March 2019, we closed on our first home in a quaint four-season vacation community in the Poconos. We cobbled together every bit of savings that we had, and I borrowed from my retirement fund so we could close on the house.

We spent two months cleaning, decorating, and preparing this house so that we could rent it out when we were not using it. Lisa painted beautiful murals in the house and in a closet space that became a reading retreat for little children. We found used log furniture and decorated every room with a log cabin theme because the outside of the house was log siding. We bought a hot tub on credit and redid the basement as a game room. Two months after purchase, the house was paying for itself because we had a continuous flow of renters.

The real gift from the house came to us during the pandemic, although it was another gift that Lisa had to be convinced to receive. As a result of the pandemic and the rush of New Yorkers seeking to escape the house arrest conditions that were forced upon them, property values were skyrocketing in the immediate areas surrounding New York. In summer 2020 when I caught wind of this, I told Lisa that if this was true, we seriously needed to consider selling the house that we had just purchased. Lisa was reluctant to discuss this. She had always dreamed of having a house in the mountains that she could rent out as a host, and it seemed as though I was stepping on her dream. As the reality of our possible move from New York became more clear and the house value continued to climb, Lisa became more open to the possibility. In December 2020, one week before I would officially accept the call to become the new pastor of St. Stephen, Longwood, Florida, we sold the house for more than double what we paid for it twenty months earlier. The enormity of this gift and blessing cannot be overstated. We were able to pay off all of our debts while having money left over for a down payment on a house when we arrived in Florida. It was clear again to us that God was at work in many ways in our lives.

To facilitate the move to St. Stephen and to help the congregation be more open and trusting in the aftermath of their challenges, the bishop arranged for me to come to the church on a two-year *term call*. A term call is for a fixed period of time, with evaluation points built into the agreement, in case either the pastor or the congregation does not feel like the arrangement is a good fit. In a normal call process, a church is given a list of several candidates who are interviewed by the call committee, and then, after some visits and other engagements, one name is suggested to the congregation to be elected to serve as the permanent, tenured pastor. This normal call process can take months or even years to complete. In my case with St. Stephen, time was of the essence. The bishop was afraid that if the church went too long without a permanent pastoral presence the existing issues could boil over into a full-fledged crisis. Therefore, only my name was given to the church. No formal call committee was constituted. The church's leadership board handled the entire process, and the decision to call me under these circumstances moved forward quickly. It was only a matter of two months from start to finish.

Upon my arrival at St. Stephen, Longwood, I could see that the church was openly hostile and divided from each other for several reasons. The national presidential election had just come to a close, and the church reflected the sentiment of the nation. Covid still loomed. Several internal congregational squabbles over wearing masks, seating during services, singing songs, and every other issue that could be debated regarding the pandemic continued. Many in the church were at odds over the style of the church services. Unfortunately, these types of issues are far too common in churches that have come through a time of dysfunction and challenge. At St. Stephen, these issues were magnified by needless debates on social media and the manner in which the last pastor exited the church. The church was far away from being a sanctuary. It had not been, or felt like, a safe place for several years. Before the pandemic, the church was losing members at an alarming rate; obviously, the pandemic didn't help.

There was lost trust in the pastoral office because of what transpired with the prior pastor. The remaining staff were on the verge of burnout and were wrestling with many scars as a result of the dysfunction of the last several years. It was my job to quickly bring stability back to St. Stephen. It once again needed to be the safe place and sanctuary that God called the church to be in this broken world filled with sin and chaos.

During those first few months at St. Stephen, I found myself preaching several pointed and strongly worded sermons that called out some of the bad behavior and having hard conversations with church members about their role in the church. I repeatedly found myself pointing to the identity that God placed upon us in Baptism as that which unites us. In a world where we increasingly point to labels to identify or discriminate against one another, our Baptism into Christ makes *child of God* the highest and most important label that we have in our lives. This label of *Christian* is a label that should predominate over all the other labels that too often tear us apart and divide us as God's creation. The label *child of God* is more important and powerful than liberal or conservative, Republican or Democrat, white, black, Hispanic, rich, poor, gay or straight, or whatever else we sling at each other to tear down. That label of *Christian* recognizes that we are not perfect and that we do not have all the right answers. It acknowledges that we are broken and sinful, and left on our own, we have no hope. Our *Christian* hope is built solely on the cross and resurrection of Jesus Christ.

Fortunately, by God's grace, and with a great deal of loving patience, the churning waters of hostility slowly began to calm at St. Stephen. This was accomplished by pointing over and over again to God's grace-filled presence and love coming to us through the gifts of the church. My goal was to make God the center of the church again by gathering around the liturgy of Word and Sacrament. The more we did this, the better the attitude and atmosphere surrounding the church became, and once again the church was returning as a sanctuary.

Adding to some of the tension and difficulty surrounding St. Stephen at the time of my arrival was the church's administration of its early childhood center, *Stepping Stones*. The school had opened eight years earlier and had relied on the church to supplement its financial health and existence. The challenges brought by the pandemic increased the tension and furthered the divide between St. Stephen Church and Stepping Stones. When I arrived at St. Stephen, the school felt like the unwanted stepchild in a relationship. There was little crossover between the church and school. Enrollment in the school at the time of my arrival lingered in the upper thirties.

Having years of experience as a pastor serving churches with schools, I immediately set out to make over the entire atmosphere surrounding the school. We began inviting the school director to give quarterly talks at our church services. I challenged the school to find more money to hire the best staff possible while empowering the administration to make necessary staff removals as soon as possible. Most importantly, we intentionally clarified the mission that Stepping Stones was a Christ-centered place that was safe for children and their families.

Within two years, enrollment at Stepping Stones moved from the thirties to nearly one hundred students. We increased and leveraged classroom space to meet that capacity. We hired the best staff in the area. Now regularly, school families are seen in the church, and church families are sending their children to the school. An unforeseen but welcome blessing that resulted from all of this is that the school is now not only self-sustaining but also helping to share in the church's mission to the community.

Within six months of my arrival at St. Stephen it became apparent to the church as well as to me and Lisa that this was a good fit. We didn't need the entire two years to decide whether or not the arrangement should be permanent. Not only were things going well at the church, but things were going also very well for Lisa. Just nine months after our arrival in Longwood, her dream came true when she was hired to work at Walt Disney World. She found her perfect job in the recreation department where she could go around and visit with families by making magic with them and playing with pixie dust. She had found the perfect job for her playful, whimsical, fun-filled personality.

By the end of my first year of service, we put in motion the necessary steps to finalize my call to St. Stephen. At our congregational meeting in May 2022, the vote was held affirming and making permanent my ministry. On October 15, 2022, the bishop came to St. Stephen to officially begin the church's fiftieth anniversary year activities by installing me as the pastor. It was a joy-filled day. All four of our children were gathered together in Florida for this special church service. They each participated in the liturgy. The congregation applauded and many members were crying as the bishop pronounced the words officially appointing me to the position.

Until the day I die, I will remember my installation day, not only because of the joy of my installation and how God had worked through the process to bring us to where we needed to be, but also because, earlier that day, with my family all together, I received a certified letter in the mail, informing me that my father had passed away.

Chapter 14
What Is Easter Hope?

In the years after I had served my parents with the order of protection after the birth of Hunter in 1998, life had moved forward for me and my family. There were occasional angry outbursts from my parents who, right before the death of my grandmother, had moved to Pennsylvania. When we heard from them, it was usually in the form of a message or letter that angrily blamed my sister and me for how badly we had treated them and what disappointing children we had turned out to be. On occasion, my father would reach out in an attempt to emotionally manipulate us during one of the times that my mother was hospitalized.

By October 2003, most contact with my parents had dissipated. I learned that my mother had died while attending a pastor meeting with my colleagues in February 2004. The new pastor of St. Paul's, Amityville, a colleague, off-handedly offered me condolences on the death of my mother. Right there in front of several of my fellow pastors, I embarrassingly learned that my mother had died the previous October.

I'm sure that my father accomplished what he desired in embarrassing me or catching me off guard. In the weeks after my mother died, he wrote a letter to my home church of St. Paul's, Amityville, asking them to pray for him, even though he hadn't been to church in decades. He knew that eventually, word would uncomfortably reach me that my mother had died. He could have taken his energy and written a letter to me or my sister, but my father's cowardly anger and venom would not allow him to act that way.

I wouldn't hear from my father again until I was going through my divorce in 2008. Since I am a public figure who is easily found on the internet, my father knew something was going on when he could no longer Google® me at St John's, Sayville. He sent an email reaching out to me to see if I was OK. In the midst of all the emotions and the chaos that was my life and family at that time, he caught me off guard and vulnerable.

I have observed during my life and ministry that no matter the depth of dysfunction and pain that may be present in a family, children always desire their parents' approval and attention. Even after all of those years, the desire to have a relationship with my father still burned deep inside of me. So, I accepted my father's invitation to meet for lunch and talk.

The lunch went better than expected. We talked about the intervening years. I filled him in on my divorce and the family. I shocked him by revealing that his oldest grandson was gay. By the end of the lunch, we made arrangements to reintroduce the grandchildren to him.

Several weeks later I took the children to his house in Pennsylvania and we spent a few hours together over a meal. It was an awkward visit. On the way home, the children and I decided that this was not anything that we wanted to do on a regular basis. My father's house was very much like my childhood home. It was messy. There were piles of items and useless objects everywhere we turned or attempted to sit. The house had probably not been formally cleaned since it was built.

Over the next year, I had occasional contact with my father. I kept our contact limited. The intensity of the situation surrounding my divorce proceedings and my need to care for the children, while rebuilding my life and career, left little time for anything else. I also did not want to get sucked back into an unhealthy codependent relationship in which my father would feel free to call and ask me to travel the two plus hours to Pennsylvania to help him.

Around the holidays in late 2010, I received a panicked phone call. My father was hospitalized for a broken ankle, requiring emergency surgery to fix it. The condition of his house had become so bad that he slipped and fell over the piles of stuff strewn everywhere. After the emergency medical technicians saw the condition of the house when they responded to his 911 call, they informed the hospital social worker. Staff at the hospital decided that he would not be allowed to return to his home until after the house was cleaned and no longer hazardous.

The following weekend, Lisa and I traveled to Pennsylvania. We stopped first at his house to see what condition it was in. After going into the house by myself, I would not let Lisa come in, what I found horrified me. There were stacks of dirty, half-eaten, Hungry Man® dinner trays piled on the kitchen sink and counter. The flies were so thick they looked like a fog over the kitchen. The refrigerator smelled of rot the second the door was opened. Mouse droppings could be seen everywhere. Moving out from the kitchen, there was no evidence of the original flooring of the house anywhere. I couldn't figure out where my father had fallen because it could have happened anywhere in the house.

We went directly from the house to the hospital where my father was recovering. He begged us to help him get the house in order so that he could go home. He would not be going directly home. He had to go into a rehab facility for several weeks before he would have the strength to care for himself again independently (though the question could be raised whether or not he ever had the ability to care for himself).

I let Lisa take the lead on this one because I was too emotionally attached and stung by this whole situation. She repeatedly asked my father if he understood what he was asking us to do. She painstakingly explained to him what our involvement would look like. She spelled out for him that we would be disposing of a large majority of the things that created the mess that caused his accident. In his desperation to get what he wanted, he willingly agreed to everything that Lisa spelled out. He was extremely reticent and cooperative. I should have known better.

On Martin Luther King Jr. weekend 2011, all six of us set off to Pennsylvania on the mission of rescuing my father. Harrison, Samantha, Mackenzie, and Hunter dutifully worked alongside Lisa and me to get in order just a small portion of the house. We spent three long days cleaning the kitchen, the living room, and my father's bedroom. It took Samantha and Mackenzie nearly five hours to empty, clean, and disinfect the refrigerator. While cleaning up the living room, I found my mother's ashes on top of the fireplace with stacks of garbage piled on top of her. Harrison, Hunter, and I lugged over seventy large industrial-strength garbage bags down to the community dumpster. With all this, we only began to make a dent in the house. At least another two-thirds of the house was left untouched and uncleaned.

Lisa was assigned to the task of cleaning my father's bedroom. When I began cleaning the room on the first day we were there, I uncovered a whole corner of the bedroom with boxes stacked with countless containers of heavy-duty prescription drugs. To say I was triggered would be an understatement. When Lisa said that they needed to be thrown out, I had to leave the room. I knew that, when my father discovered that the drugs were gone, there would be hell to pay. Lisa ordered me to leave and told me she would take care of all of it.

While cleaning the room, not only did Lisa come across mouse droppings, but she repeatedly uncovered the remains of dead mice in various places around the bedroom. She repeatedly tried to scrub clean the bathroom sink, shower, and toilet, but the dirt stains were so deep that the once-white fixtures remained a shade of brownish yellow.

By the end of the weekend, we had accomplished enough that the main areas of living where my father would travel were good enough to pass the social worker's inspection later that month. Before we left the house, I made it my mission to go into the basement and grab some important memories from my childhood. I had a feeling deep down that this may be my last trip to my father's house. I grabbed a box of family photos. The only other thing that I wanted was the set of Nikko Christmas plates and accessories that were such an important part of my childhood Christmases.

My father was allowed to return home the first week in February 2011. Within seventy-two hours of his return, he was on the warpath over all the things that were missing from the house. Most especially, he was livid about all the drugs that were missing. When I told him that they were expired and had been thrown away, he erupted. I begged him on the phone not to do this again, but it was to no avail.

Two years later, just as I was beginning my new tenure as the pastor of St. Paul's, East Northport, Lisa and I were served court papers. My father was taking us to court in Pennsylvania for *stealing* all of his stuff. If it wasn't so sad, it would have been hilarious. The children felt betrayed and were angry. At this point, Samantha was a senior in high school and wanted to come with us to the court date.

When we arrived at the courthouse in Pennsylvania a

few weeks later, I couldn't refrain from laughing. I thought the courthouse itself was a joke. It was just a small, broken-down old house in Bushkill Township. My father had hired a lawyer. We represented ourselves.

My father took the stand and proceeded to explain how we took advantage of this poor old, sick, broken man and stole all his stuff while he was hospitalized. He had an itemized list of all the things we allegedly took, all the way down to a paring knife. At the top of his list was his camera. Now we did have his camera. In the midst of our cleaning the house on that weekend mission, Mackenzie, who had taken an interest in photography, asked him if she could borrow the camera and he allowed her. After he pulled his temper tantrum upon his return home, we never had the chance to return it. What is interesting to note is that the one true item that I did steal, the Christmas plates, were nowhere to be found on his list.

After he left the stand, it was my turn. I didn't need to say much to the judge because, unknown to me at the time while we were cleaning the house, Lisa took before, during, and after photos. Her intention was to preserve the memory of what we accomplished as a family together during that weekend. Little did she know that they would be the most important evidence exhibit in the court case.

After explaining the weekend to the judge and showing him the blown-up before-and-after pictures, the judge quickly excused himself to his chambers. Initially, when he went to his chambers he had hoped to find a law that would allow him to dismiss the case because the statute of limitations had expired, but he was unable to do that. Therefore, he needed to render a verdict. When he returned to the courtroom he said, "This is a case of no good deed goes unpunished." He dismissed the case, ruling completely in our favor.

On the way out of the courtroom, I flagged down my

father's lawyer. I made arrangements to return his precious camera and I told my father's lawyer that she was to instruct him that he was to never contact me or my family ever again. That would be the last time I would see or have contact with my father on this side of heaven.

Over nine years later when the certified letter from Pennsylvania arrived on the day of my installation at St. Stephen, I knew what it was before I opened it. I just needed confirmation. The letter contained a release from my father's power of attorney regarding the liquidation of his assets. My father had died in a nursing home on (ironically) Father's Day eighteen months earlier. He chose a neighbor who was inheriting all of his stuff to be the power of attorney.

The letter was a gift and a relief. I firmly believe that this was another one of those *divine coincidences*. God was allowing me to be released from this painful family tragedy and saga that had followed me to every church that I served. As I was officially beginning my service to St. Stephen with the bishop's blessing, God was saying to me, "Go forth, you are free. You are with your new family now."

It was also an incredible relief that I would not be responsible for cleaning up my father's mess one last time. After the emotional upheaval of the broken ankle rescue mission, I don't think it would have been healthy for me, after all these years of healing and building a healthier life, to be dragged back literally into that mess. I'm sure that my father, in his warped way of thinking, believed he was getting the last laugh and punishing me for the last time. It was so important for him to get all his mother's stuff when my grandmother died that he must have thought I had that same mentality because we allegedly stole all his stuff on that weekend. He knew me so little that he never knew that material possessions really don't matter to me and our family. More than stuff, we love to make memories. Forever, in the midst of all the brokenness, our family has the memory of what we accomplished together on that weekend when we cleaned up his stuff.

Six months after my installation at St. Stephen, on Easter Sunday 2023, I preached the sermon "What Is Easter Hope?!" and told the story of my parents to my family of faith at St. Stephen. At the culmination of the sermon, I said the following:

"This is an interesting choice of topic for this joyful Easter Sunday, isn't it? I share this story with you as a personal reminder of why we need Easter Sunday and the hope that it brings. For sadly, not all stories in this life in this world have a happy Hollywood ending!...

I share all this with you and challenge you to look at those types of moments in your life, not to depress you today, but to do the complete opposite! It's for those moments in life that today is so important, so necessary, and so needed! This is why we need the hope of Easter Sunday! If Easter is not true, if it is just some made up story by a bunch of crazy first-century religious zealots, then life is just a cruel series of unfortunate heartbreaking moments. But I have seen too much that is good. Too many things that are right. And too many things that are "divine coincidences" to believe that we are born, we live, things go wrong, and we die! No! When Jesus came forth from the tomb on that first Easter Sunday, all those stories in our lives that have had an unhappy ending begin to be rewritten! For me personally, Easter Sunday is the assurance that the day is coming when I

will see my parents again. When I finally
get to see them again, it will be without
the sickness; without the drug addiction;
without the paranoid and delusional
behavior. When I see my parents again, we
will hug, we will cry, we will laugh, we
will be ok again. That is what Easter Hope
is all about! That is what awaits each of
our stories that have had an unhappy ending
in this life!"

The reaction to the sermon was so powerful that it caught me off guard. In writing the sermon beforehand, I was very anxious about the tone of the topic given that it was Easter Sunday. If not heard correctly, the sermon could have been very dark to some of the hearers. But I still knew deep down that this was a story that needed to be told as an example of why Easter is so necessary and important.

Several parishioners left the church with tears in their eyes, thanking me for being so honest. Some looked me straight in the eye with the knowing glint, saying to me, "I know exactly what you are talking about." It would be the reaction to that sermon that inspired me to have the courage to write this book.

I had finally come to a place personally, where I fully understood and embraced the church as *sanctuary*. I had finally worked through enough healing and overcome enough embarrassment to become vulnerable enough to fully embrace and genuinely disclose the reality of my life and family.

Chapter 15
Forgive Us Our Trespasses

The contentious saga surrounding my parents raises a central topic in the Christian faith that is often misunderstood and abused–*forgiveness*. The heart and foundation of our relationship with Jesus is that word forgiveness. The primary definition of forgiveness is the act of granting pardon or release toward someone for an offense, flaw, error, or mistake. It's an action word. It implies a connection or relationship between the parties whereby forgiveness is taking place. The entire life, death, and resurrection of Jesus, as recorded for us in the Bible, is about the Almighty's act of forgiveness for our sins, flaws, and errors. From that, as we pray in the Lord's Prayer, we are called to forgive each other, as God has forgiven us. Even though it appears that when we pray the Lord's Prayer, we are suggesting that God should forgive us because we are forgiving others, the exact opposite is what we are praying for. Due to the fact that God has forgiven us through Jesus, we are asking God for the strength to forgive others, as God has already forgiven us.

Some may read the story of my parents and wonder where the forgiveness was throughout all the moments of pain and offense. Some may question, as I have heard on occasion from someone close to me, "How could a pastor, a man of God, serve his parents an order of protection and cut them out of his life?" Such questions come from a fundamental misunderstanding of all the elements that make up the process and action of forgiveness. Those elements in church language are the Law and Gospel, which show us sin and grace.

I have seen during the course of my work as a pastor that misunderstandings regarding forgiveness have caused many a good, God-loving person to remain in a dangerous and abusive situation, all in the name of forgiveness. It has always troubled me when I see some sort of news report on television regarding a horrific court case. A criminal will be on trial for a heinous crime. Throughout the report, the viewer can see that the criminal is unrepentant and obstinate regarding the crime committed. Then the news report will flash to a relative of the victim who proclaims their forgiveness for the criminal, who has no desire for their forgiveness nor has any sense of remorse. This is *not* the full act of forgiveness. Forgiveness is relational. The relative of the victim who is proclaiming their forgiveness has a beautiful, grace-filled heart. If the opportunity ever presented itself, and the criminal repented and sought it out, forgiveness could take place. This is what we should all pray for, especially when we find it hard to let go of something bad that has been done to us. But when someone like that criminal remains defiant and unrepentant, the act and circle of forgiveness has not taken place.

Churches and their pastors, especially in my Lutheran tradition, love to dwell on the merciful, gracious, and loving Jesus, as we should. We love to talk about the passive, gracious, and caring Jesus, who is seen in the imagery of the Good Shepherd (see Psalm 23 and John 10: 11-18). But sometimes overlooked are those times when Jesus harshly and angrily condemns and stands up against those who are arrogant and abusive to others. Jesus shows unending mercy to those who are contrite and repentant. Jesus welcomes all whose unjust circumstances in life place them in situations where they are living lives that are less than ideal in God's eyes. But to those who know better, those who are in a position of power over others, those who are seemingly doing things in the name of God yet not being faithful, Jesus minces no words. When the money changers in the temple court were price gouging all of the pilgrims who traveled long distances to come to the Jerusalem temple for the atonement rite, Jesus angrily flipped their tables (see Matthew 21: 12-17). When Jesus sends out the seventy disciples to share the word of the kingdom of heaven, he instructs them that when they are rejected they are to shake the dust off their feet, which was an ancient expression of rejection and condemnation toward someone (see Luke 9: 1-6).

A proper understanding of God's Word and its teachings for us sees a distinction between what is Law and what is Gospel. The Law is summed up in the Ten Commandments. The Law of God is anything that teaches, directs, commands, and provides expectations for life and living as a person of God. The Law of God works in three ways in our lives: by acting as a curb, a mirror, and a guide. A curb keeps us in line. Curbs line the sides of roads in case a driver who is not paying attention and may be drifting toward the sidewalk will be startled by bumping the curb and redirected back in line. There are those times in our lives when God gets us back on the right path. When the Law of God acts as a mirror, it is usually to show us that we don't look so good. We have committed some sin and act that is painful and destructive for ourselves or others, and it needs to be fixed and cleaned up. The Law is a guide for us when it teaches us how to behave and instructs us toward what is better and healthier for our lives.

If human beings were born without the flaw and stain of sin, we might be able to live according to God's Law and expectations perfectly. Unfortunately, because we are all born imperfect and sinful, our attempts at keeping the Law fall short of God's will and desire for our lives. Our failure to keep God's Law is what we call sin. According to God's teaching in Romans

6: 23, "... the wages of sin is death." That's why Jesus was born outside the normal means when He was born of the virgin Mary. By being born outside the seed of a human father, original sin was not passed down to Him. Therefore, He was able to live by the Law of God and keep it perfectly. Jesus should not have had to die because He committed no sin. His death then became a substitutionary sacrifice for us. The wages of our sin were placed upon Him and He paid the price.

While God provides these words of instruction and expectation in the hopes that we live healthy and happier lives, God's desire is not to condemn us eternally and destroy us when we fail to do so. That's where the other great teaching of the Bible, the Gospel, becomes central and foundational to our lives. Romans 6:23 goes on to say, "For the wages of sin is death, but the free gift of God is eternal life in Christ Jesus our Lord." The free gift of God is what we refer to as the Gospel.

The word *Gospel* comes literally from its roots in the Greek language, "good news." When Jesus was born in Bethlehem, we hear in Luke 2:10 that the angel appeared to the shepherds, who were watching their sheep in the fields at night, and the angel announces, "I am bringing you *good news* of great joy for all the people: to you is born this day in the city of David a Savior, who is the Messiah, the Lord." The Gospel is anything in the Bible that tells us the good news that God still loves us, in spite of our sin, and seeks to love us, care for us, and redeem us from all the punishment and condemnation that we deserve as a result of our sin.

Living a healthy life of faith takes to heart both God's Law and Gospel. If the Law becomes too prominent as a source of Christian living, then our relationship with God becomes a series of rules that we must keep and perfect to earn the favor and love of God. This is, sadly, a doomed effort. Try and try as we may, because of those inherited sins and flaws that are passed on from the generations before us, we will be overwhelmingly frustrated by our failure to live up to God's Law and expectations. This often rears its ugly head when Christian churches spend most of their time pointing out all the rules that must be followed to make it to heaven and pronouncing harsh judgment on those who are struggling with sin.

The opposite problem of overemphasizing God's Law is the proclamation of the Gospel in a way that excuses an individual from having to worry about living life according to any expectations. This manifests itself with the dangerous attitude sometimes seen among people of faith when they say things like, "Well, since God loves me, I can do whatever I want, even if it is hurtful because God will forgive me." Such attitudes denigrate the enormous sacrifice of Jesus' death on the cross. This cheap idea of grace is what often causes people to remain in abusive and dangerous situations because it focuses solely on the grace and love of God while overlooking the fact that love is also manifested in rules and boundaries that are desired by God to protect us. It is also the reason that people who are outside the church often think Christians should always be kind, nice pushovers, no matter what is taking place.

When teaching young people about God's Law and Gospel, I like to talk about one of the first rules that exists in every household. When children are young, every loving household has the rule "Don't touch the stove." Especially in this day and age of glass-top stoves, one can never know if the burner was just turned off and is still hot. This rule is made by the parents out of love. It is their deep desire that their young children not break the rule and subsequently burn themselves, experiencing great pain. That is what the Law is. But inevitably, there are those children who, whether on purpose or by accident, break the rule, burning themselves. When the rule is broken and the burn occurs, the loving parent does not stand there and laugh at the child saying, "Ha, ha, you broke the rule. Now your skin is stinging and falling off." No, the good loving parent scoops up the child and does everything needed to fix the pain and heal the situation. That's what the Gospel is.

Law and Gospel work in relationship to each other. As we seek to make our way through the challenges of life in this world, the Law helps us to see the dangers and identify those things in our lives that are bringing harm. The Gospel is what rescues us, heals us, and renews us, when the Law is broken and condemns us.

In my relationship with my parents, I struggled constantly with the tension between the Law and the Gospel. My heart as their son, and my heart as a pastor, always sought to be gracious. I deeply wanted to love them and to be loved by them. I wanted to overlook their flaws and their abusive behavior and make things right again. However, in their broken condition, they were unable to live their lives in the restraint that God calls for with His Law and expectations. Rarely, if ever, did I ever experience any contrition or remorse on the part of my parents. They were incapable of applying the Law to their lives in a way that made things healthier. As a result of that, there were those times in my relationship with my parents when I had to make the difficult decision of building stronger boundaries in our relationship to protect myself and my family.

While the Law and Gospel can often be seen as matters of black and white, living faith-filled lives is more often about shades of gray. In the back-and-forth struggles of my relationship with my parents, you can see this playing itself out. When I got the order of protection against my parents after Hunter was born, that was a moment in my life with my parents when I had to set aside grace and forgiveness and instead had to act more out of the Law and the need to show them that their behavior was unacceptable. When I reconnected with my father during my divorce, that was driven by the grace and love of the Gospel and the willingness to find forgiveness in our relationship. But a few years later when my father sued us after we cleaned up his house, once again the application of the Law became necessary.

In my ministry as a pastor, I have sadly seen the confusion of Law and Gospel play itself out in the lives of many people who remain in abusive relationships. A person who is the victim of abuse will sometimes remain in the abusive relationship because they feel an indebtedness to Jesus and what the Bible says about marriage. Therefore, they remain in the relationship, hoping to offer forgiveness to the abuser. The problem with that scenario is that the abuser is most likely not playing by the same rules and, frankly, is probably not even on the same playing field.

If the abuser were sincerely living a life of faith, then the abuser would know that their behaviors were unacceptable and against God's Law and desire for life. That faith should lead to a heart that is remorseful and repentant, and the abuser should then do everything in their power to follow the repeated words of Jesus and "Go and sin no more." This should not then lead to a continued cycle of abuse where the abuser acts out, then apologizes, and then goes and does it again. True repentance is a turning around and a turning away from the behavior. To the best of that person's ability, the destructive, abusive behavior should cease.

Now of course, as broken, sinful, people, this is a lot easier said than done. That's where the grace and forgiveness of the Gospel comes into play. In each relationship, people must decide where the line lies in their willingness to continue in the relationship when the offense returns or continues. While Jesus calls us to turn the other cheek (see Matthew 5: 38-42) and reminds us to be unceasing when our brother or sister comes asking for forgiveness, when He talks about forgiving seven times seventy times (see Matthew 18), I do not believe that Jesus expects us to remain in relationships that are abusive and destructive. Before Jesus talks about forgiving seven times seventy times, He has harsh words of warning against those who hurt children and cause them to go astray. Jesus' grace is always the goal, but it is not to be used as an excuse to continue to hurt and abuse others.

Ultimately, we are called in our faith walk with God to do the best we can to live our lives according to God's rules and expectations. God knows that we are not going to live perfectly. God knows that we are going to mess up and we are going to hurt each other. God knows that there are times where we are going to have to make very hard and painful choices regarding our relationships. That's why, in the end, the message of the Gospel–that God's love for the world overcomes and is greater than all those things–is the foundation of our faith.

When we confess the great ecumenical creeds of the church, the Apostles', the Nicene, and the Athanasian Creeds, we acknowledge that God will come again to judge the living and the dead. As the Creator and Savior of all things, God is the only One who truly has the right to judge when it comes to the spiritual matters of Law and Gospel. One of the biggest problems plaguing the Christian Church in today's world is that we each spend too much time judging one another, effectively taking God's judgment out of the picture. We should each worry more about our own lives and our own actions. Each of us has enough to deal with on our own in determining how well we have each personally kept the Ten Commandments and lived in God's grace.

Jesus was once tested by the religious leaders of His time

when they asked Him what was the greatest and most important commandment. They were hoping that Jesus would choose one of the Ten Commandments. If He choose one commandment of the ten as greater than the others, they could accuse Him of blasphemy and discredit His work and ministry. But in His Divine wisdom, Jesus answers by saying, "You shall love the Lord your God with all your heart, and with all your soul, and with all your mind. This is the greatest and first commandment. And a second is like it: You shall love your neighbor as yourself. On these two commandments hang all the Law and the Prophets." (Matthew 22: 37b-40.) His reference to "[loving] the Lord with all your heart" is a reference to the first three commandments: You shall have no other gods; Do not misuse the name of the Lord God; and Remember the Sabbath Day and keep it holy. Jesus' reference to "love your neighbor as yourself" is a summation of the remaining seven commandments that all tell us how to properly interact with our neighbor by not killing them or stealing from them or coveting their property or spouse. In essence, Jesus is saying all of the Commandments are equally important because they are all about love. That's why He said, "love the Lord" and "love your neighbor."

The highest of all callings for the Christian and for the church is to love one another. As Jesus was just hours from hanging on the cross, He said to His Apostles in John 13: 34-35,

"I give you a new commandment, that you love one another. Just as I have loved you, you also should love one another. By this everyone will know that you are my disciples, if you have love for one another."

The most important behavior that reflects the heart and life of Jesus in us is not judging one another but loving one another. We should do everything we can to live by the Ten

Commandments. But the most important thing to live by is love. Healthy love lives with rules and boundaries, as well as with grace and forgiveness.

Chapter 16
Planes, Train(ing), and Motorcycles

"Hey, Friar, what's up?" is how I answered my cellphone when I saw that my dear friend Jonathan was calling.

"Listen man, I'm all right. I want you to know that I'm all right. You may see something on the news later about our plane making an emergency landing, but I'm all right."

"That's a good one man, that's funny, you got me." I replied.

"No, seriously man, we had to make an emergency landing in Heckscher Park, because we ran out of gas" he emphatically responded.

He wasn't kidding. Jonathan, who had been taking flying lessons for over eight months, had to make an engine-failure emergency landing with his flying instructor in a small state park on the southern shore of Long Island. To log more hours to qualify for his Visual Flight Rating (VFR) certification, Jonathan decided to take a two-day flight with his instructor for a quick overnight to visit his brother in North Carolina. On the way back on Sunday, April 15, 2012, just after the plane made the turn off the coast of New Jersey to line up for a landing at Brookhaven Calabro Airport, the single engine Cessna propeller began to sputter, and then it completely stopped.

The instructor told Jonathan to open his side door

completely, while the instructor did the same. This was a requirement when a crash landing was possible. They radioed an emergency SOS to the tower and prepared for what might be a wet landing into the Atlantic Ocean or, if they could glide past Fire Island, a wet landing into the Great South Bay. Fortunately, by God's grace, they had enough altitude to glide far enough that they made it to the southern edge of Long Island just past the beach shore, cleared the last tree tops that were within arm's length from the open door, and plopped the plane down in an open field in the middle of the park. Jonathan spent the rest of the day being interviewed by the Federal Aviation Administration.

The next day, as Jonathan was driving the three miles to his job at the Sayville Library, with no zoo or wilderness anywhere in sight, a kangaroo—well technically a wallaby—hopped into the passenger-side of his car, while the car was moving, and knocked itself silly. No joke. After spending hours being interviewed by the authorities the day before, Jonathan was hesitant to call the police to report the wallaby incident. He was afraid that they might have taken him to the psychiatric hospital. That's the kind of luck my friend Jonathan has. On the day after Jonathan nearly crash landed, the wallaby escaped a local home and hopped right over to the road where Jonathan was driving to work. Lisa and I suggested that Jonathan play the lottery that week.

I met Jonathan in 1997 when I first came to St. John's, Sayville, to be the pastor. Jonathan had recently returned from his college studies, and he wanted to meet with me to discuss how he felt that God had been calling him to a more significant role in serving the eternal kingdom. Jonathan is an intelligent and gifted person. He fluently speaks five different languages. He holds two master's degrees and likes to challenge himself to learn new things and to push his comfort zone, like taking flying lessons. We went to the first of what would be many lunches where we discussed life, the church, and how God is leading us to serve.

Within a short time of our meeting and building a friendship, Jonathan decided that he believed that God was calling him into ordained ministry as a pastor. Together we set out to help Jonathan discern the best path for him to get the education and credentials needed to become a pastor.

At that time in the Lutheran tradition, the basic path toward ordination for a person who felt called to ministry was that they needed to leave their current life and enter into the seminary (the graduate school that gives a Masters of Divinity degree in order to become a pastor). For Jonathan, this meant leaving his very secure job at the Sayville Library and starting over in either St. Louis, Missouri or Fort Wayne, Indiana, where the two primary Lutheran Church-Missouri Synod seminaries were located.

This was problematic for Jonathan, not just because he had a good job with great benefits, but primarily because throughout his life he had been wrestling with a serious form of rheumatoid arthritis. His chronic disease had been so challenging that it took years for him to finally find the right doctors who could treat him so that he could function normally. It required, and still requires, several high doses of expensive medications to keep his immune system in balance. The idea of Jonathan's picking up his life and leaving the immediate care of his doctors would have been a serious threat to his health and well-being.

When God calls you and has a plan for your life, it's not so easily deterred. Just look at the story of Moses, Jonah, Paul, and many of the other servants that God chose in the Bible. We tried to get Jonathan accepted into the alternate path toward ordination that our Church body was offering at the time. The program known as DELTO, Distance Education Leading Towards Ordination, was primarily a remote-learning process with occasional short classroom sessions for a week or two at a seminary. This program would have been perfect for Jonathan. Those in charge of the program, however, were only open to accepting students who were already integrally involved in a church's ministry, such as cross-cultural ministry or a rural church where it is hard to find and keep a pastor. For a student coming from New York, that at the time had an abundance of pastoral ministry, there was no need to make an exception for Jonathan.

Of course, this was a great disappointment that for a period of time deflated Jonathan's journey toward ministry. But remember, God is not easily deterred when God has a plan for our lives. Not long after this rejection Jonathan came to me with great excitement. He found an extension of The Southern Baptist Theological Seminary in Louisville, Kentucky, that offered weekend classes in New York City, where he could eventually get a Master's of Divinity degree. In addition to the weekend classes, he would have to go to Louisville for two weeks, twice a year, for intensive classroom study and evaluation time.

This was a very different path for the typical Lutheran pastor. When Jonathan completed the requirements for The Southern Baptist Theological Seminary, he would then have to take more classes in the Lutheran tradition to be ordained as a Lutheran pastor. Jonathan was on board for all of this.

Over the next ten years, from 1999 to 2009, Jonathan faithfully took his weekend time and vacations from the library and did all the necessary work to obtain the required Master's of Divinity degree. This meant that he would leave his job at the library on Friday afternoon and take the train into the city for his three-hour Friday night session. He would sleep over in the guest dorm and then attend class all day on Saturday with the professors who flew up from Louisville, coming home late on Saturday night. He would then wake up on Sunday morning to serve at St. John's. As part of this process, to give him the practical experience and hours that he needed to fulfill the Lutheran requirements, in 2005 I consecrated Jonathan as a deacon for St. John's.

Jonathan carried a heavy load during this time. He worked full time at the library and then would often be up late at night completing the reading and assignments needed for his weekend classes. When he had an extra moment, he would make visits to the sick in the church with me and help with other pastoral duties. I was blessed during all this time to grow closer to him and to call him my friend. We shared our deepest struggles and sought out together God's direction and consolation.

When my marriage fell apart in 2008 and I resigned from St. John's, Jonathan remained a true friend and one of the only people that I was close to who truly, like Jesus, walked with me. He was often that little gift of grace and assurance that I needed as everything else was seemingly falling apart. When Lisa and I got married in early 2012, Jonathan presided over the wedding at Transfiguration, Harlem.

After I left St. John's, Jonathan was left under the direction of my former assistant pastor who was not as supportive of Jonathan's journey. I think this pastor felt that Jonathan was taking a second-class path toward ordination and would not be as fit or qualified for a future position in the Lutheran church. He tolerated Jonathan's completion at Southern Seminary, but he did not overwhelmingly support Jonathan as he completed his studies.

Upon completion of his degree, Jonathan spent the next

few years jumping through the hoops necessary to fulfill the requirements to become a pastor in the Lutheran Church-Missouri Synod (LCMS). He had coursework in readings of Lutheran theology that he had to complete before he could pass a theological interview that would then allow him to be certified for ordination.

In 2013 he had finally satisfied the requirements. He was under the belief that when he did, now fourteen years later, that the pastor at St. John's, Sayville, would welcome him to be his part-time pastoral assistant. Unfortunately, the pastor sabotaged a potential call to St. John's, because, in my opinion, my successor seemed threatened by Jonathan.

By this time, I had become the pastor of St. Paul's, East Northport. I didn't hesitate to swoop in and scoop up my gifted friend Jonathan. Not long after I came to St. Paul's, I moved the congregation to accept Jonathan as the church's newest deacon until we could sort through the necessary steps so that he could now be ordained in the other Lutheran church, the Evangelical Lutheran Church in America (ELCA).

Like the LCMS, the ELCA also has its own set of requirements that need to be met to be certified for ordination. Traditional theological questions need to be answered, but the ELCA is more concerned about the psychological and mental health of potential pastoral candidates. Therefore, Jonathan went through some additional time and waiting as he was evaluated for ordination in the ELCA.

Finally, on my forty-sixth birthday in 2016, nineteen years after the beginning of Jonathan's journey to becoming a pastor, I had the privilege of preaching the sermon at his ordination service at St. Paul's and then, along with the bishop, laying my hands on him as he was ordained into the Holy Ministry. In the sermon I preached, I started by telling the story of his emergency plane landing and used the theme "learning to fly" to talk about how it may not have been the original flight plan that Jonathan had filed, but God still was his co-pilot to get him where he belonged.

I have the utmost respect and admiration for Jonathan and his deep faith. Most people, including myself, would have become so frustrated by the systemic requirements and all the setbacks that Jonathan experienced that we would have given up on the journey. Jonathan did not give up. God never wavered and never gave up on Jonathan, even when the flawed human servants overseeing the process could neither get out of their own way nor God's.

Jonathan was part of God's bigger plan for my life and journey as well as St. Paul's, East Northport. After I left for St. Stephen, Longwood, Pastor Jonathan took over the primary duties as the pastor. He has faithfully served them, on a part-time basis, since I left. He is awaiting the day when he can retire from the library and offer his immense skills to the Lord's work on a full-time, daily basis.

Jonathan's life and call to the ministry are another example of how God works to make his church a *sanctuary* even in spite of the roadblocks and selfish impediments that sinful human beings sometimes throw in God's way. The church is not a perfect place, but ultimately God is the Lord of the church, and God gets what God wants, in God's time.

Like so many other times in my life, watching God's timing in Jonathan's journey was a lesson in patience. But God always knows when the timing is right. Jonathan was not meant to be a pastor in the LCMS. They did not welcome him and his gifts the way they should have. They did not appreciate the potential for diverse multicultural ministry that he could offer through his language skills. They did not make the church a *safe place* for his ministry. In God's time, at the right time, after God got my ministry back on track, God called Jonathan to where he belonged. It was because of all this that I had the confidence of knowing that St. Paul's would be OK after I left because God led Jonathan there at the right time.

Today, for someone who may feel called to ministry, many more open and welcoming paths to become a pastor are available. Gone are the days where a pastoral candidate has to stop and pick up and move somewhere new. Now many seminaries, especially in the ELCA, will consider all the circumstances of one's life and potential ministry and do everything possible to get out of God's way. There are alternate remote paths to ministry certification that may allow a future pastor to remain in place while studying. If you are considering offering your life in service to the kingdom of God, have a conversation with a pastor and pray that God's timing and presence will guide your direction.

Oh, by the way, if you are wondering, though Jonathan doesn't fly much anymore, and who can blame him, he is still learning and to do new things. Now, he has taken up motorcycling. Lord have mercy.

Chapter 17
Don't Blame God for the Church's Mess

When he grew annoyed and frustrated, my Uncle Bill was often overheard saying "People suck!" It was his way of reminding himself to have low expectations anywhere people were involved in something. His saying, "People suck," was a simplistic way of acknowledging the sin that manifests itself in our lives. The problem with the Church is that it is made up of people. Where there are people, there is sin, and yes, sometimes, people suck. According to our scriptural point of view, all people are sinners and imperfect. Therefore, wherever people are, mistakes are going to happen, sins are going to occur, and people are going to get hurt. It is sinful people throughout the Church's history who have brought about the problems and divisions that have tarnished its reputation and made it more difficult for the Church to do the job that God has called the Church to do.

In recent history the institutional Church has been in the midst of a public relations nightmare. Various research studies show that the majority of Americans still have a high positive opinion of Jesus. Depending on the study, anywhere between seventy to over eighty-five percent of Americans still see Jesus in a positive light. But when it comes to the Christian Church as an organized institution, research indicates that the Church's reputation is in deep crisis. Some studies indicate that Americans view the organized Christian Church in the same manner that they view the United States Congress, with favorability ratings below twenty percent. This is a contributing factor to why there are so many people today who say that they are *spiritual* but not *religious*. Such language is a direct reflection of their views of the organized Church.

When we are honest about the stories that have come out of the Church over the last few decades, we can see that this public relations crisis is very much a self-inflicted wound. From the repeated scandals of the televangelists to the revelation of the sexual abuse of minors, the inability of Church leaders to manage themselves and the Church in a godly manner has deeply afflicted the faith and trust of so many who had formerly looked to the Church to fulfill their spiritual needs.

This is heartbreaking and cause for great concern. The Church has seen the need for repentance and continues to have to do everything in its power to be a sanctuary in every sense of the term. Throughout the history of the organized Christian Church, there have been times when the Church has made mistakes and committed sins that have done more to harm parishioners than carry out the Lord's commission to make disciples. Yet, in spite of such sin and dysfunction, God is still at work through the Church and, it is important that we distinguish the work of God from some of the things that happen because of the people in the institutional Church.

But as much as people are the problem, people are also the reason why the Church is still vital and necessary in today's world. The primary purpose of the Church is to bring God's grace, love, and forgiveness to broken, sinful, hurting people. Even though the Church is made up of these broken, sinful, hurting, and, sometimes, sucky people, God still incredibly and miraculously works through the Church and her imperfect leaders to give people the love and grace that they desperately need.

Throughout my ministry I have observed that there is a

perception problem when it comes to the Church's mission and identity. This is reflected in all of those times when a well-intentioned Christian says something like, "I don't need to go to Church to worship God, I can pray to God on my own, or at the beach, or in the beauty of nature." Such statements may acknowledge the beautiful work of the Creator's hand, but those statements indicate a complete misunderstanding of why the Church exists and why the Church is necessary.

The word *worship* is defined as "paying homage our praise to a divine or supernatural being." Such a view of worship puts the individual as the actor and God as the receiver in the midst of the spiritual relationship. The Church advertises its worship times. The Church talks about its worship and praise music. This is *not* what the Church is about. Though the word *worship* is used in Church language all the time, I feel it creates a false impression of what the mission and the identity of the Church is all about because it implies that we who go to Church are the primary actors when it comes to what is happening in Church.

For the Church to most effectively carry out her mission and identity of making disciples and bringing God's grace and love to people, the Church must be a place where God is the primary one doing the work. Church is a place where God serves people with love, grace, and forgiveness through the gifts that are at the center of the Church's work. These gifts of God, which can also be called *Means of Grace,* are the sacred Scriptures and the blessed Sacraments.

One of the most important verses in my understanding of my role as a pastor is Romans 10:17. St. Paul writes, "So faith comes from what is heard, and what is heard comes through the word of Christ." People often say to me, "Pastor, I want to have faith" or "I want my faith to be stronger." It is that verse and the principle it teaches that offers the answer to the questions when people are searching for a deeper faith. Faith is not an intangible cosmic wave that we by happenstance connect to. According to the Bible, there is a specific cause-and-effect manner in which faith comes into our lives. The more we hear, read, and receive the Word of God, the more faith comes and is strengthened in our lives. Therefore, the primary responsibility of the faithful Church leader and of the Church is to make the Bible (the Word of God) central in everything that the Church does. In the aftermath of Jesus' resurrection, St. John summarizes the point of the Gospels, as well as the whole of Scripture, when he states,

> Now Jesus did many other signs in the presence of his disciples, which are not written in this book. But these are written so that you may come to believe that Jesus is the Messiah, the Son of God, and that through believing you may have life in his name. (John 20:30-31 NRSV).

As the Bible is read and proclaimed in sermons, songs, and prayers, God is speaking to people. When God speaks to people, our perspective on life and what really matters is changed. Worship and praise on the part of God's people is an appropriate response to receiving God's presence and power as the Word is heard, but worship and praise are not the primary identity and purpose of the Church's work. In essence, the work of the Church is an ongoing conversation with God. God speaks to us first, creating faith. We respond with our prayers, praise, and worship and with offerings of our time, talents, and treasures. This conversation and relationship begins and ends with God's work through the Gifts of the Church.

The Sacraments are an extension of the Word of God. Throughout the Bible, God has worked through visible, tangible, earthly things to bring the assurance of the Divine presence and Divine grace into the lives of the people. God appeared to Moses in the burning bush. The Son of God appears in the fiery furnace to Shadrach, Meshach, and Abednego. When Jesus came into the world, He literally became the God that people could touch, hold, and listen to (see John 1:1-14). As He walked around and spoke as the living Word of God, He commanded that the Word of God, with the blessings that it brings, be attached to water in the gift of Baptism and to bread and wine in the gift of Holy Communion. How wonderful it is that God chose such simple and easily available gifts to connect His grace and love to the people!

These gifts of Baptism and Holy Communion are Divine, holy actions of God, not because they make sense to us rationally and scientifically, but because God has spoken in Scripture that specific things are attached to these earthly, tangible items, and something happens when these Sacramental Acts are performed. Romans 6: 3-5 NRSV says,

> Do you not know that all of us who have been baptized into Christ Jesus were baptized into his death? Therefore we have been buried with him by baptism into death, so that, just as Christ was raised from the dead by the glory of the Father, so we too might walk in newness of life. For if we have been united with him in a death like his, we will certainly be united with him in a resurrection like his.

Those words show that Baptism is something more than a mere symbolic pledge. Those words show how Baptism intertwines the baptized to the resurrection of Jesus. It is God's assurance that in Baptism, the Resurrection is given to the baptized.

When Jesus was hours from His sacrificial death on the cross, He took the bread and the cup of wine and said, "This is my body" and "This is my blood, given and shed for you for the forgiveness of sins. Do this in remembrance of me." In the original Greek used to record the New Testament, the word used for "is" has only ever been translated as "is," not "represents" or "symbolizes" or "could be." There are no alternative translations. Clearly, as these words were recorded by the Gospel writers, they intended to capture the concept that the Lord's Supper was more than a symbolic meal. It is the presence of Jesus, and when it is received, forgiveness and grace are received with the bread and wine.

From these Scriptural teachings, the Sacramental practices of the Church, especially in regard to Baptism and Holy Communion, have been a central and foundational part of the Church's mission and purpose to the world. For the sin, brokenness, and pain of human beings to be overcome and healed, the presence of God needs to enter through Word and Sacrament. For the Church to be a sanctuary (remember a *safe place*), the presence of God bringing grace, love, and forgiveness must come. This presence of God comes through the Scriptures and water and bread and wine.

Though this should have always been the central focus and foundation of the Church's work in history, sadly, because of the sinfulness of human beings, other motivations and misunderstandings have crowded out these things leading to the sins and mistakes that have divided the Church into all the denominations that we have today. At this point in history, there are estimated to be anywhere between thirty thousand and fifty-two thousand different Christian denominations in the world. Most of these divisions are a result of sinful human beings arguing and disagreeing about the things of God.

God is not happy that the Christian Church is so divided in today's world. In John 17:11 (NRSV) Jesus prays right before dying on the cross, "Holy Father, protect them in your name that you have given me, so that they may be one, as we are one." Jesus went to the cross the next day to be the healing sacrifice for all the division and brokenness brought by sin. I am sure that it was not His intention to die so that through the centuries the Church could continue to commit sins that would further divide God's people.

The many denominations that mark the Christian landscape today each have their own stories and reasons why they disconnected from some other Christian body. Many of these stories have good reasons that are grounded in trying to preserve a better understanding of God and God's work in the world. But all too often those original reasons for division are lost and forgotten as history moves forward and other motivations take over the motivations of the Church bodies.

The New Testament book of Acts tells of the first few decades of Christianity following the death, resurrection, and ascension of Jesus. The first two centuries of the Christian Church existed within the landscape of the Roman Empire. At different times during this history, the early Christians were met with varying levels of tolerance or oppression. The Roman emperor considered himself a god to be worshipped by the people. Therefore, any religion that was monotheistic, like Judaism and Christianity, which taught that there should be no other gods, was not easily tolerated. Some Roman emperors were more accepting of the early underground movement of Christianity than others.

In the late 200s AD, Constantine rose to Emperor and by 313 AD decreed in the Edict of Milan that Christianity was no longer illegal in the Roman Empire. This brought Christianity out into the open and set the stage for the time later in that century when Christianity would become the official Church of the Roman Empire. As a result of this, birth was officially given to what we know today as the Roman Catholic Church.

Throughout the remainder of the first millennium, there was basically one Christian Church that expressed itself in two halves. The western part of the Church in the Roman Empire is what we know as the Roman Catholic Church. The eastern part of the Church, centered in Constantinople, would become known as the Orthodox Church. In the history following the Edict of Milan, any debates and conflicts that arose within the Christian Church were addressed in large gatherings of all the Church's leaders known as *ecumenical councils*. There were seven of these ecumenical councils held from 325 AD to 787 AD. The councils determined the basic fundamental beliefs of Christianity. The Creeds that confess who God is as Father, Son, and Holy Spirit were the results of these councils. The dates of Christmas and Easter were determined by these councils. Debates about correct teachings were all the work of these councils. The main purpose of these councils was to bring unity to the Christian Church while removing everything that would undermine the Church's mission to bring the presence of God to the world.

For the most part, the first eight hundred years of Christian history moved along keeping the Church mostly united, bringing much growth to the Church numerically and geographically. But as things moved toward the beginning of the second millennium, human imperfection and the temptation of power began to crack the foundation of the Church. In 1054 AD, in a dispute over the power of the Roman Bishop, also known as the Pope, the two halves of the Church permanently split and condemned each other. This *Great Schism* as it has become known would set the stage for the earthquake that would come five hundred years later.

In the centuries following the Great Schism, leadership within the Roman Catholic Church became more driven by politics and world-order issues than by theology and questions about God. As the Roman Empire became weaker, the Roman Catholic Church grew in power, stature, and influence. As with most earthly institutions, the growth of power, influence, and wealth can bring with it greater temptation toward weakness, corruption, and sin. The crusades brought the use of violence to the forefront of the Church's work. In the late 1300s, three different men were fighting over Papal authority and power. The construction of St. Peter's Basilica brought the selling of indulgences into the Church's practice of redemption. Indulgences were pieces of paper sold by the Church to gain forgiveness for oneself or for loved ones who had died. The income from indulgences became a primary source of income for the Church. As a result of all of this, by the early 1500s, there were many within the Church, and outside the Church, clamoring for change.

Martin Luther was a Roman Catholic priest who grew increasingly frustrated with the Church's practice of indulgence selling. On October 31, 1517, Luther hammered his *95 Theses* on the door of the Castle Church in Wittenburg, Germany. These 95 Theses were his invitation to the leaders of the Roman Catholic Church to discuss and debate the growing concerns regarding the direction and leadership of the Church. It was Luther's hope that the Church would correct course and get back to focusing upon Jesus's redeeming work above all else. It was not Luther's intention to begin a new Church body and divide the Church. Unfortunately, due to forces inside and outside the Church, Luther's desires were rejected.

The resulting fallout from that moment in history ushered in what is known as the *Reformation*. The Christian Church would be forever changed and divided from that moment forward. Those who followed Martin Luther became known as the Lutherans. Other Christian branches followed Huldrych Zwingli in Switzerland and they became known as Reformed Christians. In France, John Calvin gave birth to Calvinism which led to Churches in the Congregational,

Reformed, and Presbyterian traditions. At the same time in England, in a dispute over his many divorces, King Henry VIII broke the English Church away from the Roman Catholic Church, giving rise to the Anglican and Episcopal traditions. The unity that had been held by the power of the Roman Catholic Church quickly came undone. The result, over the five hundred years leading us to today, has been both a blessing and a curse to the work of the Christian Church on earth.

The past five hundred years since the Reformation have continued to bring division within Church bodies, bringing about all the denominational labels and separate branches that characterize the Christian Church today. While these divisions are the result of the brokenness of sinful human beings, that does not mean that God is not at work in these various expressions of the Christian faith. Too often these divisions are not respected for the different ways that God can work in the world in reaching people, but instead these divisions are seen more as badges of honor as to who can better represent Jesus and who is more right about God than others.

This is the sad reality of broken, imperfect human beings being the leaders of the Church and the vessels by which God works in the Church. Where there is sin, there is division and brokenness. But remember, this is exactly why God works for us and comes to us. The beauty of God's grace is that God works in, through, and in spite of sinful, broken people.

Though the Church is divided because of the sins, abuses, and controversies that have arisen throughout her history, the Church finds her unity in the main mission and purpose that is found in Jesus Christ. As God comes into the Church in the blessings of Word and Sacrament, even with all the different denominational labels, the Spirit of God brings healing and unity that will be eternal.

As much as I lament that the Church is broken and

divided, I rejoice that God is still working in all these different expressions of Christianity when the gifts of God's Word and Sacraments are present. Fifty days after that first Easter, when Jesus rose from the dead, and ten days after He ascended into heaven, the miracle of the Pentecost took place. Suddenly, the Holy Spirit descended like fire on the disciples giving them each the gift to speak foreign languages that they had never spoken before. Without having to spend years getting an education to learn another language, in an instant, those disciples were given the ability to go to people outside their normal comfort zone and culture and share the good news of Jesus' love and forgiveness (See Acts 2: 1-13).

That is what the power of God's grace is all about. Even though sin divides and breaks apart people, God works to bring unity and healing. Yes, the Church is somewhat of a mess because of the sins and mistakes of human beings. And unfortunately, many people who attend Church find themselves getting hurt in Church by the sins of others because people can suck and do sucky things. But the Church is God's place that welcomes sinful, sucky, broken people who need healing. In Matthew 9:12-13 NSRV, Jesus says, "Those who are well have no need of a physician, but those who are sick. Go and learn what this means, 'I desire mercy, not sacrifice.' For I have come to call not the righteous but sinners." The Church is a place for sinners because God is present in the Church to heal and help sinners. The Church will never be a perfect place. But the Church is, and always will be, the perfect place for imperfect people. Therefore, a sanctuary.

Chapter 18
From a Certain Point of View

In *Star Wars: Return of the Jedi,* after Yoda reveals to Luke Skywalker that Darth Vader is indeed his father, Luke has a moment where he meets with the Force Ghost of Obi-Wan Kenobi and questions Obi-wan as to why Obi-wan lied to Luke about Luke's father's death. Obi-Wan explains that Anakin Skywalker, Luke's father, ceased to exist and thus became Darth Vader, in essence killing his father. Obi-Wan then doubles down by saying that what he said was true "from a certain point of view."

With that exchange, George Lucas, the creator and producer of the original Star Wars films, who was deeply influenced by his study of world religions, captured what is often the point of contention in religious divisions. The various denominations that have arisen throughout the course of Christian history have done so because of *a certain point of view.* The large majority of Christian bodies see the Bible as the inspired Word of God. But the extent to which they go in seeing what is authoritative and how it is interpreted comes from a certain point of view.

The issues that led to the birth of the Lutheran Church over 500 years ago are no longer prevalent in the Roman Catholic Church. Since the 1960s, the Roman Catholic Church has enacted reforms that were the result of the Second Vatican Council that addressed many of the issues that caused the need for the Reformation. The liturgy of the Mass is no longer spoken in Latin but is now spoken in the common language of the people making it easier for "faith [to come by] hearing... the Word of Christ." The Roman Catholic Church has become more open to recognizing the other expressions of Christianity while entering into ecumenical dialogues aimed at healing some of the divisions of the past. Unlike the time when indulgence sales were central to the Church's work, the gracious sacrifice of Christ is once again foundational in the work and proclamation of the Roman Catholic Church.

Yet, for all the progress that has been made, there are still issues that exist between Lutherans and Roman Catholics, as well as Lutherans and other Lutherans. Most of these issues arose from having a certain point of view. For the purposes of this book, I will primarily address some of the differences among the Lutheran bodies.

For Lutherans, the Bible is the inspired Word of God that is authoritative for all that we believe and confess. But even among Lutherans, there are different points of view as to how that inspiration determines what we believe and how we practice our faith. Though there are hundreds of different Lutheran Church bodies in the world, since I have been a pastor in both the Lutheran Church-Missouri Synod and then in the Evangelical Lutheran Church in America, I will limit my comments to these two. The LCMS and the ELCA represent the two largest Lutheran Church bodies in America.

For the Lutheran Church-Missouri Synod, the Bible is the inspired, inerrant Word of God in its original form, meaning the Hebrew, Aramaic, and Greek. The idea is that when God's Spirit entered into the life of the prophets, apostles, and other human authors that God used during the writing of the Scriptures, that God got what God wanted and God meant what was said and written. The primary means of interpreting and understanding what is written in the Bible is through what is called the *Historical-Grammatical* method of interpretation. In this approach to understanding the Bible, the original language words are analyzed by how they have been historically used and understood and by how the form and tense of the grammar reflected meaning at the time of writing. Cultural and societal factors are given less consideration.

A classic example of this approach to the Bible comes from the Creation account at the beginning of Genesis. When Moses authored and compiled the first five books of the Bible, the Hebrew word "yom" was used to refer to each of the "days" in which God worked creating the universe. The LCMS interpretation of this is that because that word *yom* in its original Hebrew commonly referred to a standard day (24 hours) at the time of Moses, then God created everything in the universe in six standard days and rested on the seventh day.

Such an approach is used throughout in understanding what the Bible says from the LCMS point of view. Because God got what God wanted and God says it like God meant it, Scriptural passages are to be interpreted from mostly a literal point of view.

The Evangelical Lutheran Church in America also confesses that the Bible is the inspired Word of God. The approach to interpretation however follows more of a *Historical Critical* approach to the Bible. While still respecting the Bible as the Word of God, this approach takes into consideration the context of the world, the culture, the audience, and the time that the words were written, in addition to how the original language words were commonly used and interpreted. This approach takes into account that the Bible includes things that can be considered scientific or historical but does not necessarily assert that the Bible's discussion of such things is not open for debate.

For instance, the ELCA's approach to the creation

account in Genesis does not hinge on how long it took for God to create the universe. Though creation is mostly considered to be a scientific topic, the Bible is not about scientific authority. The most important thing about the creation story for our faith journey is that God created the universe by the power of His Word in the beginning. How God created the universe and how long it took do not matter in the big picture when it comes to what is really important in our faith.

Many of the divisions that exist within Christianity are the result of arguments over issues of interpretation of the Bible that have little to do with the primary reason and purpose of the Bible, which is to believe that Jesus is the Savior and to have life in His name. When we confess our faith through the historical Creeds of the Church, all we say about creation is that God created the heavens and the earth. The wisdom of the church, at the time those Creeds were authored and put into the church's practice, knew enough not to dwell on the particulars, but to just keep the main thing the main thing. God created the universe. Sin made it a mess. Therefore, Jesus entered into the creation through the flesh of His mother Mary, so that God could fix the creation that was broken.

Sadly, there are many divisions in the church's history that have come from cataclysmic arguments about secondary issues, such as how long God took to create the universe, that have overshadowed the primary mission and work of the church to make disciples of all nations. This tendency to debate such issues often loses sight of the fact that we are fallen, imperfect beings that cannot and do not understand all things.

A problem with a strong fundamental and literal approach to interpreting the Bible is that we are working from a disadvantaged point of view in the first place. While the Bible may have been perfect in its Divinely inspired original form, we do not have any part of the Bible in its original, first edition, signed form. When we seek to interpret the Bible today, we are working with copies of the original language text, several generations removed from the original writing. Until the invention of the printing press in the 1400s, the Bible was copied by hand, leaving much room for those scribes to change and add to what the Bible originally said. You can find examples of this in most English Bibles today by looking at the ending of Mark's Gospel where Chapter 16 has two different endings or the beginning of Chapter 8 of John's Gospel. There is usually a note saying that the story of the woman caught in adultery is not in the oldest and most reliable manuscripts.

Additionally, when every word in the Bible is given equal authority and emphasis in how the word was used and interpreted at that time, it leaves less room for consideration of the historical and cultural factors that surrounded the Biblical writers at that time. For the ELCA, this is very important in our approach to the role of women in the church. There are passages in the Epistles of Paul that say that a woman should not preach in church when those words are interpreted solely on the linguistic characteristics. The LCMS takes those words as authoritative and restrictive to a woman holding the position of a pastor in the church. In addition to Paul's words, the ELCA takes into consideration the context and the audience to whom the words are being written. There was an early church controversy surrounding false teachings about Jesus that were being spread at the time of Paul's writing. These heresies were often being promoted by certain women preachers, quite possibly influencing the words that Paul chose. This raises the question as to whether Paul's words were a permanent admonition to the church or whether they were time related?

In promoting women to the pastoral ministry, the ELCA also relies on the many examples in the Bible of women in leadership roles, especially during the ministry of Jesus. The first and primary witnesses and proclaimers that Jesus had risen from the dead were women. Though the argument is often made that Jesus did not choose a woman to be one of the twelve apostles, by understanding the deeply patriarchal society structure that existed at Jesus' time, it could be understood and interpreted that if Jesus had chosen a woman to be one of the twelve apostles, it could have discredited and stood in the way of the most important thing–spreading the message of His love and grace.

That is at the heart of the ELCA's approach to understanding the Bible and practicing the Christian faith. The Bible is ultimately about Jesus. The central point and theme that ties the Bible together is the promise that the Savior the world needs is coming, and Jesus is the one that is promised. Therefore, Jesus is the lens through which everything else in the Bible is seen, interpreted, and understood. It is this approach that enables the ELCA to proudly welcome all to receive God's grace and love. There are certain passages in the Bible that seemingly condemn same-sex relationships, but there is scholarly debate as to what exact sin those passages are condemning, based upon the cultural context of the time. Today, the need to see and receive the grace and love of God in Jesus is more important than anything else.

It's not that the ELCA sees the Bible with less respect than the LCMS. In fact, I believe that the opposite is true. The Bible is so important and influential, because of the life and love of Jesus, that it is acceptable for us to dig deeper behind the scenes to understand the context, the methodology, and the manner in which the Bible came together. Because Jesus is the center of the Bible, it's not an issue if the books of Moses came solely from Moses' hand or if there were several different hands whose work Moses then gathered together in the books attributed to him. It does not matter if there are seeming contradictions in the details of stories in the Gospels. Different people focus on different things when telling a story. What matters is that Jesus is the center of the story and the reason for the story.

During my time as a LCMS pastor, I would often find myself doing things that I believed were the right decisions when it came to caring for the people that God had entrusted to me, but I was worried that doing such things would get me in trouble within the LCMS. The LCMS is so concerned about correctly interpreting the Bible that they present the idea that LCMS pastors should not work cooperatively with other Christian traditions that do not share fully in what the LCMS believes.

One time while I was at St. John's, Sayville, a grandmother of one of my members was a Roman Catholic and was killed by a drunk driver. The funeral was held at the Roman Catholic church. During the funeral, I fully vested and served on the altar alongside the Roman Catholic priest. I also took communion in that church with the family. This was the right thing to do for the family during their time of crisis and loss. This was a humble approach to the grace of God in a broken world. But this decision, along with many other decisions like it, could have gotten me suspended or removed from the LCMS if word ever made its way to the wrong leadership.

My time serving as a pastor in the ELCA has allowed me to breathe more freely when it comes to making pastoral decisions that are best for the needs of serving God's people. The ELCA understands and celebrates that it is just one expression of Christianity in the midst of the many different ways that Christianity is confessed and practiced. In word and action, the ELCA understands that we are all broken sinners who need God's grace and that we are all just doing our best to make our way through this world, while clinging to the robes of Jesus.

Chapter 19
Ministry in Extraordinary Circumstances

Pastoral Ministry can sometimes feel like being a firefighter. A pastor is called upon to be most active and present when an emergency is taking place. When someone falls unexpectedly ill or dies suddenly, a Church that has a healthy and trusting relationship with their pastor will find members are comfortable enough to immediately inform and call upon the pastor to be present with the assurance of God's grace and love.

Unfortunately though, because sometimes those emergencies can come fast and furiously, being a pastor can feel like being a firefighter because we are moving from one emergency to the next. I often want to go back and check up on the family of the last emergency but find myself lamenting the reality that I am needed at the next crisis and am hard pressed to go back to the previous crisis.

While leading Church services, preaching sermons, and teaching Bible classes are the main part of a pastor's vocation, a pastor is most effective and connects best with their parishioners when the pastor is available, reliable, and present when hardship and trauma come home personally in the lives of the people.

Most of the time, a pastor is called upon to serve individuals and families at times of crisis. But there are times during a pastor's ministry when there are challenges and difficulties that effect the entire Church community and require the pastor's attention in addressing the needs of the whole family of faith at the same time. September 11 was certainly one of these moments. As of late there have been two global challenges that have profoundly challenged the Church as a whole, as well as my personal pastoral ministry.

The Sars Covid-19 Pandemic was unlike any challenge that the Church and her pastors have had to face in over a hundred years. The velocity and intensity in which Covid arose in our parishes left every pastor scrambling for answers and solutions as to how the Church could still be a sanctuary for people who were afraid to, or unable to, gather together.

At most times in human history when there was some type of local or global challenge that effected an entire Church, the Church was able to do its job by gathering together around God's gifts and prayer. The Covid-19 pandemic countered all the ways that the Church would normally be empowered to do the things that God has called us to do. History has shown that when there is a major event like a war, or September 11, or the death of a prominent historical figure, Church attendance increases in the time during and after those events.

In the case of Covid-19, Churches were shut down by local authorities and governing Church bodies out of concern for not contributing to the spreading of the virus. I certainly would love to say much about those decisions and how they were handled but that does nothing to further the purposes of this book. My goal here is to share how the Church found a way to still be a sanctuary in the midst of the exceedingly challenging circumstances that existed during the time of the pandemic.

The week that the pandemic officially hit the New York area was the second week of March 2020. Thursday, March 12 of that week marked my twenty-fifth anniversary as a Lutheran pastor. A special catered luncheon had been planned for the following Sunday. As the news of the pandemic kept getting worse and as, bit by bit, the New York metro area was shutting down, it became inevitably clear that we would have to cancel the celebration. As it turned out, the services we held at St. Paul's, East Northport, on that Sunday morning would be the last Church services that we held in person in the Church building for eight months.

For the first several weeks of the pandemic, St. Paul's did what every other Church was forced to do. We recorded our service with just the pastors and the organist in the Church sanctuary. During this time, many Churches were forced to quickly develop a way in which they could video record their services and disseminate them to their parishioners, who were not able to come to Church.

Throughout my ministry, I had some semblance of a video ministry that helped me reach out with the Gifts of God, and this prepared me well for the pandemic. From my time as a child when I sat at home and listened to the Church services through the phone because of the issues with my parents, I had learned to be aware that there were children of God who could not always come to God's house to be fed by God's Word. Therefore, I welcomed and promoted alternate means by which God's blessings could be brought to the people.

During my years at St. John's, Sayville, we had an official video ministry team. A camera person operated a tripod camera from the Church's balcony. The feed from the camera went into six VCR recording machines, all lined up in a cabinet, simultaneously making six videotapes. In the days following, those six tapes would be taken by a team of Church members to local nursing homes and to members who were sick and shut in at home. When a person did not own a VCR to watch the service, the Church purchased a VCR for that home.

By the time I was called to St. Paul's, East Northport, video recording of Church services and sharing them had become much easier due to the evolution of technologies such as smartphones, YouTube®, and mass-market email software. During my time at St. Paul's, I would place my iPhone® on a gooseneck holder centered on a Church pew a few rows back. When I stepped up to read the Gospel lesson and preach my sermon, I would hit the record button on my Apple® watch. As soon as the service ended, I uploaded the recording to my YouTube® page and emailed the link to the entire Church email list.

This practice set us up for what would be needed during the shutdowns of Covid-19. When the pandemic hit, we expanded our recordings to film the entire service. Unfortunately, because we could not gather in person, there was no opportunity to receive the Lord's Supper. Therefore, the recorded services contained the readings of the day, the pastor's message, one or two songs, and the prayers of the Church. (When I arrived at St. Stephen, Longwood, the church had already invested in a high-quality video system and computer. They didn't have just one camera. Their system was so fancy that three different cameras were enabling different angles with the ability to zoom in and out and change the perspective depending upon what was taking place in the Church.)

By the end of May 2020, it became apparent that, at least in New York, there was no end in sight to our inability to gather inside in person for our Church services. Growing increasingly frustrated with the situation, I was determined to find a way that the Church could still be a sanctuary for the people who desperately hungered to be together as Church in the midst of this terrible, anxiety-provoking situation.

St. Paul's was blessed with a beautiful large open field on the campus behind the school building. At the far end of the field was a small, six-foot-high hill. As I looked out over the hill in those days in late May, I could envision having an altar on top of the hill and inviting Church members who felt comfortable enough to bring their lawn chairs for a brief Church service where they could also receive the Sacrament of Holy Communion.

From Memorial Day weekend through the Sunday before Thanksgiving 2020, St. Paul's held a Church service outside in the midst of the pandemic. We continued to video record the service for those who remained at home. Attendance fluctuated between sixty and a hundred attendees. There were only two Sundays when the weather was a concern. By Thanksgiving weekend, it had become too cold to continue to gather outside. But by this time, some of the restrictions regarding indoor gatherings in New York were beginning to loosen, and we moved the service back into the Church sanctuary. Most of the parishioners who had been attending the outdoor service continued to join us when the service moved inside.

The hardest and most frustrating aspect of being a pastor during the Covid-19 pandemic was that the Church was restricted from doing its job as a sanctuary in the midst of a global issue that regularly reminded people of their mortality. It's at those moments that the Church is needed the most. When the Church was forced to shut down, the people of God were left to deal with these threats without the assurances that could be found in the Church. My calling as a pastor is to do everything in my power to make God's gracious and loving presence available to people, all the time, but especially in the midst of a worldwide crisis. I hope that never again in my ministry I will have to deal with such obstacles in bringing the presence of God to the people.

The political environment that has surrounded us over the last few years is the other global issue that has profoundly affected my work and ministry as a pastor. The divisive rhetoric, the incessant need to name-call and label, and the demonization of others from the opposite political party, have sadly slithered their way into the Christian Church.

Throughout my ministry, I have always worked very hard to make the Church a safe, neutral place when it comes to political issues and agendas. This does not mean that I do not address and talk about hot-topic political issues. My goal is to address them first and foremost from a Biblical, Christ-centered perspective, without coming too close to a particular party's agenda. For this reason, throughout the majority of my ministry, I have registered myself as an independent voter. I feel that this allows me to look at and address political issues without feeling loyalty to a specific political party and agenda.

It is my firm belief and my pastoral goal when I am leading a Church to make sure that who we are as believers in Jesus is the highest and most important of all the labels and identifying markers in our lives. The Church, and by Church I mean every Church that gathers around the grace and forgiveness of Christ, must be a place that is safe (a sanctuary) for all people of varying backgrounds. It is the grace and love of Jesus that should enable us to be together as a family of faith, while still acknowledging and accepting that we come from different cultural, economic, social, and political backgrounds.

The Church has existed longer than any earthly government or political structure. The mission and work of the Church goes far beyond the issues and limitations of this world. Therefore, the Church must be an entity unto itself. It exists and works in this life in this world and should be a powerful force of influence for the way we live in this world. But the Church must always keep its eye on the kingdom that goes beyond this world, the kingdom that is eternal.

This is why, especially in the midst of a personal crisis as well as global issues, we need what the Church offers even though the Church moves to a time and rhythm all its own. The Church marks time and identifies its existence in this world through things that point to the life and the world to come.

The Church gathers around a calendar that is different from the secular calendars that mark our years. The *Church Year* counts time by marking the important events and teachings in the life of Christ and the work of the Church. The first half of the Church year moves the people through the birth, life, ministry, and death and resurrection of Jesus. The second half of the Church year focuses the Church on how to best live as a Christian, knowing what Jesus has done to love us and save us.

For each of the movements of the Church year, there are appointed Bible readings from the Old Testament, the Gospels, and the New Testament letters that give to each season, week, and holy day a specific message and theme that, hopefully, strengthens our faith and trust in God, while leading us to live holier lives, according to what God has said is best for us.

This system of readings, known as the *lectionary*, repeats itself every three years. The idea of this is that those who go to a Church with a tradition that follows the Church year and uses the lectionary, will be exposed to a large majority of what is written in the Bible. This supports the concept presented by St. Paul in Romans 10:17 when he told us that faith comes by hearing the message of Christ Jesus.

When a Christian practices their faith in a Church that utilizes the Church year and lectionary and comes to Church every week for three years, that person will hear almost all of the four Gospels, just about the entire New Testament, and many of the most important and key stories in the Old

Testament. This reinforces how God is the one speaking and at work to create and strengthen faith.

The Church year and the lectionary manifest themselves with their benefits in the historic liturgy of the Church. The historic liturgy of the Church is a gift that has been passed down through the many centuries of the Christian Church's existence. It helps to bring us the life, ministry, and presence of Jesus, while uniting the Church in a certain way, even though we are sadly divided by all those sins and debates that have led to all the labels and names that are on our Church signs. Lutherans, Roman Catholics, Episcopalians, and other Christian traditions that use the liturgy, when they gather for Church, are united around the foundation of Christ, even though history has divided us.

The movement of the Church service begins by reminding us that we need to be in Church because we are sinful and we call upon the name of the triune God given to us in our Baptism. We cry out to God as so many of the faithful called out to the Lord for mercy throughout the time of the Bible. We are reminded that God came into the flesh when Jesus was born through Mary and the angels sang "Glory in the highest" when the shepherds were in the fields. We hear the words of the Bible point us to Jesus and His work for us in the lessons of the day. We are taken to the moment of Jesus' victory as He entered into Jerusalem on Palm Sunday and the crowds sang "Hosanna" to Him. We are reminded that He died for our sins to save us when He became the "Lamb of God." We are joined to the resurrected Jesus and His promise to us, when we receive the resurrected body and blood of Jesus in the Sacrament of the Altar. Like those early Church disciples, we are sent forth after we have met again with Jesus, through the liturgy, to "Go in peace and serve the Lord."

When we gather in the repetition of this movement that

God brings to us through the liturgy, the lectionary, and the Church year, we are receiving from God everything that we need to deal with all of the extraordinary personal and global issues and crises that this sinful, broken world throws at us. When we gather in the grace, love, and presence of God through these gifts, in this fashion, we are empowered to deal with the challenges that are before us, while being reminded that our hope and our lives go beyond the things and the problems of this world.

In this life, marked by sin and the pain that it brings, things will never be perfect. But gathered together around God in the gifts of the Church, we find sanctuary, especially in the most difficult of times.

Chapter 20
May the Force be with You

Obi-wan never told you what happened to your father.

He told me enough. He told me you killed him.

No. I am your father.

No. That's not true. That's impossible.

Search your feelings. You know it to be true.

Nooo. Nooooo.

As a ten-year-old boy, seeing *Star Wars: The Empire Strikes Back* on the third day it was released into the movie theaters in May 1980, that moment seared into my very heart and soul.

I was already a huge fan of *Star Wars*. Three years earlier in the summer of 1977, my mother took me to see the original *Star Wars* movie. The following years were marked by unending joy when it came to that movie, especially at Christmas, because I would open the newest *Star Wars* figures and toys. By the time the next movie came out, going to movies like *Star Wars* had become a culture phenomenon and event. I remember lining up for hours in the ticket line outside the theater waiting for our show time to come. When more *Star Wars* movies were released in the late 1990s and early 2000s, I would pass the tradition on to my own children. We would wait for the midnight showing on opening night of the newest film to be released.

The waiting time between *The Empire Strikes Back* and the conclusion film of the original trilogy, *Return of the Jedi*, felt like an agonizingly long wait. The years between the ages of ten and thirteen can feel like forever. As you grow to be an adult, three years of time flies by in an instant. But as a young boy, three years can be torturous, especially when you are waiting for the answers to some of the most important questions in life. Is Darth Vader really Luke's father? Who is the other hope? What will happen to Han Solo? Will he be frozen in carbonite forever?

But it wasn't just the joy of the entertainment that sucked me in. The spiritual tones found throughout the *Star Wars* story, especially being connected to the "force," as well as the redemption story found between Luke Skywalker and his father, Darth Vader, resonated with me on many levels, even as an immature, prepubescent teen. As already witnessed by the account of my father's arrival at the LuHi sports awards dinner, I was wrestling with my relationship with my father. When Darth Vader declared "I am your father" to Luke, I believed it could be real, because, in some ways, I saw my father in the same type of light. But when Luke saved his father by the end of *Return of the Jedi*, that moment became the defining moment of hope as I continued to grow up in our broken, dysfunctional household.

The redemption of Darth Vader lined up perfectly with the stories of redemption through the Son of God, Jesus, that the sanctuary of the church was teaching me. Even the language of the *Star Wars* stories lined up with the language of the church. In church we hear and say, "The Lord be with you." In *Star Wars*, it's "May the force be with you." For me, as I grew up, the force of God and the force of *Star Wars* walked hand and hand.

Throughout my ministry, illustrations, themes, scenes, and references from *Star Wars* have helped me to convey the message of Christ to the churches that I have been called to serve. I have preached about Darth Vader and Luke's relationship. I have used Yoda and his famous phrase "size matters not" to teach about faith. On one Easter, I used the digital resurrection of *Grand Moff Tarkin* in the movie *Rogue One* as a lead-in to my sermon. And don't think that I haven't been tempted to substitute "The Lord be with you" with "May the force be with you" instead.

This love of *Star Wars* was not limited to only the movies and the toys. In my adulthood, just as I was beginning my training to be a pastor at the seminary, books continuing the *Star Wars* story began to be published on a regular basis. From that day forward, my escape from the pressures of preparing for the ministry, and then during my time as a pastor, would be marked by a temporary excursion into the world of *Star Wars* through the many fantastic authors who continued the vision of George Lucas. The books explored the themes of good versus evil, the power of the force, the temptation of the dark side, and how love sacrifices for others, in a depth and detail that the movies could never capture. Even the most minute of characters and throw-away story lines in the movies found new life in the world of literature.

When Disney® purchased the rights for *Star Wars* from George Lucas in 2012, I found myself struggling with mixed emotions. I was filled with excitement and anticipation that new stories and movies would be forthcoming. I was, however, also a little ticked off that all of the books that I had read, probably totaling over a two-thousand-dollar investment on my part, would now be considered "legend" and no longer a true part of the *Star Wars* story. I wish that Disney® had taken a little more care and interest in how they handled the literature.

But I also understand that when there is a four-billion-dollar investment at stake, the small market section of book readers is not a primary concern.

For the most part, I have been pleased and thankful for what has happened with the *Star Wars* story since Disney® took over. Unlike many of the things I see on the internet, I am not one of those fans who looks for things to complain about and criticize. I appreciate how each new *Star Wars* movie, TV show, and book fills me with feelings of anticipation and nostalgia as their release comes near. I still go to the earliest showings of the movies when they are released in the theaters. I get up early in the mornings when a *Star Wars* show premieres on the television.

Of the more recent works of *Star Wars*, the movie *The Last Jedi* was met with very sharp and critically mixed reactions upon its release. But personally, the more I let the movie sit with me and the more I thought about its main plot point, the more I found myself again appreciating the spirituality of the saga. In *The Last Jedi*, Luke Skywalker has gone into hiding. Everything that he thought and believed when it came to the *force* and the *Jedi* has been called into question. He has been betrayed by one of his students, his nephew, to whom he was close. The happy ending that was the redemption of Darth Vader has now been overwhelmed by the return of darkness and evil in the galaxy.

Much of the criticism surrounding that movie was the portrayal of Luke Skywalker as a beaten, dejected hermit, instead of the conquering hero that we were left with at the end of *Return of the Jedi*. But for me, especially through my personal journey as a pastor, Luke's predicament was not far-fetched. During the time of my divorce, and as I struggled to find my way in the midst of Harrison's sexuality revelation, I experienced similar feelings to those that were attributed to Luke in *The Last Jedi*.

Sometimes, the Christian faith can be presented in a way that leads to the idea that, as long as I give my life to Jesus, everything is going to be great. Life is going to move along in a prosperous way. My efforts and investments are going to be blessed. My prayers are always going to be answered the way I hope and want them to be answered. This type of theology is often seen during the messages of TV evangelists and in churches that proclaim what is often referred to as "prosperity Gospel." This is not a full, genuine presentation of the Biblical message of Christianity.

Christianity is not an agreement with God that everything in life in this world is going to blessed, right, and perfect. At the heart of the Biblical message of Christianity is a recognition that life in this world is broken and marked by sin. Yet, we look to Jesus Christ by faith to guide and lead us through the challenging times, knowing that we are not alone. In *Star Wars* terms, this would be looking to the "force" as the dark side comes near. Christianity does not guarantee prosperity in this life. Christianity looks to the hope that is yet to come in the resurrection to life everlasting.

Most of the great servants of the Bible, especially those closest followers to Jesus, did not find perfect, prosperous lives, where they died comfortably in their sleep, after they met Jesus. The majority of the Apostles and early church servants endured torture, prison, and terrible deaths. What they did find and have after they encountered Jesus was a new way to see life in this world. They obtained a peace and courage that empowered them to not fear, even in the most horrific and challenging of situations. They found comfort in their Christian community that helped them find their way through adversity while often offering solutions together to the problems that sin created. Most importantly, those early Christians found the ability to believe in redemption and second chances when life went in the wrong direction.

When we try to put our expectations on God and the world because of our faith, we can often find ourselves disappointed and disillusioned. This even happens to Jedi masters and to pastors. The biggest internal conflict that I had to come to terms with throughout my life was how I, a pastor, could have such a broken and dysfunctional family. When I deflected the topic of my parents and hid the pain I was feeling, it was because I was falsely living under the idea that, as a person and a leader in faith, this should not happen to me. In reality, I truly came to understand and embrace my faith and who I was when I realized that my faith in Jesus is exactly for these broken things. The "force" of Jesus' love, grace, and forgiveness is given to me through the sanctuary of the church to lead and guide me through the dark side of things to the light of the life to come.

By the end of *The Last Jedi* Luke's new student reminded him what his faith as a Jedi was all about. Luke returned from his exile to offer his life as a sacrifice to save the ones he loved. Throughout my ministry, at those times when I struggled with challenging emotions, losses, and disappointments, it has been my parishioners, those who I have been called to serve, who have often served me and reminded me of what Jesus' sacrificial love is all about.

In church, we may not say "May the force be with you," but when the pastor says, "The Lord be with you" and the people of the church say "and also with you" or "and with your spirit," there is a force at work more powerful than the world has ever seen. The light and power of Jesus has conquered the dark side of sin and death.

Chapter 21
Wrestling with God

In January 1984, the Iron Sheik entered Madison Square Garden as the World Wide Wrestling Federation Champion. In the aftermath of the Iranian hostage crisis, the Sheik was the epitome of the evil bad guy. He waved an Iranian flag with the face of the Ayatollah painted in the center. He wore the keffiyeh and sneered as the people booed. A month earlier the Iron Sheik won the title when he schemed and cheated to intentionally hurt the shoulder of the former champion, Bob Backlund.

In the face of this looming threat to pro wrestling, New York City, and international affairs, a new hero had just arrived in town, fresh off his appearance in the movie *Rocky III*. His name was *Hulk Hogan*. As he entered the Garden to the blaring sound of the song *Eye of the Tiger*, the fans in attendance stood to their feet and rocked the arena with their cheers.

At the apex of the match, it looked as if Hulk Hogan were about to lose. The Iron Sheik had him cinched in the dreaded *camel clutch*. He rocked back as he sat on Hulk's back, seemingly causing great pain to our hero. But, in a moment never seen before when the Sheik had that move locked in, Hulk Hogan stood up and ran backward banging the Sheik into the corner. He then tossed him to the mat, dropped his leg on the Sheik with the force of his three-hundred-pound body behind it, and to the count of one, two, three, Hulk Hogan became the new champion.

From the moment when I was ten years old and my

invalid grandmother first showed me professional wrestling on television, I have loved the grandeur, spectacle, and the over-the-top-ness. I have loved the larger-than-life characters like Hulk Hogan, Andre the Giant, The Rock, Stone Cold Steve Austin, and the Tribal Chief Roman Reigns. I have loved the story lines and the athleticism.

I'm such a big fan that Lisa and I have traveled to different parts of the country to take in the biggest wrestling event of the year, Wrestlemania®. We have seen this annual "Superbowl of Wrestling" in places like New Jersey, Dallas, Orlando, Tampa, and Philadelphia.

Yes, I know the ending and the finish of a pro wrestling match is predetermined. This has often been the object of the public's scorn in saying that professional wrestling is fake. But it is the fact that the endings and outcomes are predetermined that has been such a source of joy for me. Pro wrestling can be another form of escape from the struggles of life. Most of the time, the good guy wins or overcomes the obstacles in the way. What is so appealing to me about this art form of professional wrestling is that it is the consummate story of the battle of good versus evil. In the end of a good professional wrestling story, good triumphs over evil, just like our faith in Christ.

As we hear about the fall of Adam and Eve in the Garden of Eden, we hear how the Bible sets up the eternal wrestling match between good and evil, God and the devil, heaven and hell. In Genesis 3:15, we hear God say to the serpent, within the ear shot of Adam and Eve, the following: "I will put enmity between you and the woman, and between your offspring and hers; he will strike your head, and you will strike his heel."

Behind the scenes, good guys in pro wrestling are known as *faces,* and bad guys are known as *heels.* I have researched the origin of these terms regarding pro wrestling good guys and bad guys. I even have a neighbor whose son-in-law is a professional wrestler and asked him about the term. There is no clear origin story of the terms heel and face, but the themes conveyed and played out in pro wrestling certainly feel like they could have found their meaning by alluding to these opening words of the Biblical story.

From that moment of promise in the Garden, the Bible is leading us to better understand who will come to strike and overcome the head of sin and death. We know today, because we have the entirety of the Bible to show us, that Jesus carried out this long-foretold prophecy by being the face of God wrestling with sin and death on the cross. The head of sin, evil, and death was crushed eternally at that moment. But the heel of Jesus was struck and hurt because He had to die in order to achieve it.

My love of pro wrestling goes beyond what we see on TV. I love, and have loved for years, the behind the scenes of the business and how the story threads together week to week. I like to hear how the matches and storylines are developed leading to the moment when the hero, the face, prevails over the heel. I want to know what goes into the physicality and the building of emotions that are conveyed in the matches.

Though the wrestling matches are scripted, and the outcomes are predetermined, there is nothing fake about the athleticism needed to succeed in pro wrestling nor is there anything fake about the risk of injury. Professional wrestlers are professional athletes who train as hard as any other athlete in sports. Watching wrestling inspired me to take better care of my health and body.

Growing up in the 1980s, I was immersed in the health and body development craze that was embodied in pop culture media. Lou Ferrigno as the Hulk, Sylvester Stallone as Rocky and Rambo, and Arnold Schwarzenegger as the Terminator, in addition to my love of pro wrestling, helped me to develop a mindset that I needed to take care of my body.

From my teen years, I have taken seriously the need to train my body and intentionally sweat as often as possible. Motivated by not wanting to become what my father was in life, I started lifting weights in high school. By my late teens, I also started doing aerobic activities like jogging. This has continued throughout my life, right up to today. Now in my fifties, I walk (with my dog) four miles on six mornings a week. I usually skip Sundays because I have to be at the church very early. At least four to five days a week, I hit the gym for weight training.

Throughout my ministry, I have been motivated to take care of my body by what I have witnessed my parishioners endure. I lament how often I have had to visit and minister to people who are hurting or hospitalized because they have not taken care of their bodies. In 1 Corinthians 6: 19-20, St. Paul reminds us,

> "Or do you not know that your body is a temple of the Holy Spirit within you, which you have from God, and that you are not your own? For you were bought with a price; therefore glorify God in your body."

Fully living a healthy life according to the Word of God is doing everything that we can to live in body, mind, and spirit. In the same manner that we study and learn to strengthen our minds and go to church to empower our spirit, living fully by God's intention means taking care of our physical bodies as well. Living by God's design means not taking our bodies and their health for granted.

I am increasingly alarmed by the general state of health that I witness in our country today. Due to sin and the imperfection of the world, there are enough threats to our health from disease and things outside of our control that we do not need to further complicate and jeopardize our health by not taking care of the things that we can control. Understanding that we are a "temple of the Holy Spirit" should encourage us to do what we can to live healthier lives physically by getting exercise, eating less processed foods and sugars, and doing what we can to avoid putting unhealthy chemicals into our bodies.

Our calling as people of faith is to, wrestle with God, figuratively and literally. We wrestle with God's Word and will for our lives and our work here in this world. We wrestle with our baptismal identity, who we are, how we live, and what we do as we present ourselves to the world around us. We wrestle with sin and temptation as it relates to God's grace and forgiveness. We wrestle with our mortality as we anticipate the fulfilment of the promise of everlasting life. We wrestle with our bodies and our health. We wrestle with the flesh and the spirit. We wrestle as both sinners and saints. We wrestle with God's direction for our lives while wanting to do our own thing.

When a professional wrestling match is put together and scripted, the finish of the match and who will win is determined first. It is then up to the participants in the match to tell the story of how they get to that finish. Wrestlers engage in what is known as *selling*. Their facial expressions, their moves, their pain, their joy, their shock, are all parts of telling the story on the journey to the finish.

This is very much what living life as a Christian is like. By our faith connection to Jesus' death and resurrection, the end of our story is already written and predetermined. As we live our life, it is up to us to write the script and sell the story on the way to the finish.

This is what holy living is all about. Having the assurance that we are not alone and that nothing can conquer us when Jesus is on our side, we are called to do the best we can to live a life that reflects the story of Jesus and the outcome that is promised to us. Therefore, our faith is not like an insurance policy that we hide away in a drawer until there is some tragedy and we have to pull it out to enact it. We are called to live the story as much as we can each day by selling it in our words and actions.

Good works have always been associated with practicing the Christian faith. In the early church, we hear in Acts 2: 44-45, "All who believed were together and had all things in common; they would sell their possessions and goods and distribute the proceeds to all, as any had need." Throughout the centuries, the Church has intentionally worked through educational institutions, healthcare centers, relief organizations, and immigration services to carry forth the love of Jesus by living lives that tell the story that God loves the world.

These holy efforts and good works are not just the responsibility of the organized, institutional church. Each of us, as individual parts of the body of Christ, play a role in selling the story each day and getting to the finish. One of the first songs that I remember learning in church as a small child back in the 1970s was entitled "They'll Know We Are Christians By Our Love." While the song reflected the folk style of church music that was popular at that time, the message is enduring. Love is at the heart of our Christian identity. It should be a part of our story, not just on Sundays, but all the time.

The biggest obstacle to the health and the growth of the Christian church today is the charge of *hypocrisy*. The word finds its origin in the Greek word for *actor*. Today, the word hypocrisy implies that you say one thing and do something different. This rarely is intended as a compliment. When the word hypocrite is directed toward the church, it usually means that the actions of the individual Christian or the Church as a communal body are not reflective of selling the story as Jesus would want it told.

While our good works and holy efforts are not what save us and bring us eternal life, they do reflect what Jesus means to us. They affect how others perceive the church and what it does in the world. There should be an attitude of appreciation and indebtedness that is communicated in our daily living that sends the message that our relationship with the Almighty, through the saving work of Jesus Christ, has changed us and changed how we live in the world.

In response to what Jesus has done for us and how Jesus blesses us by what is given to us in our lives, we are encouraged in our faith walk to give back to the world in our actions. The church uses the language of giving our time, our talents, and our treasures for God's work in the world. When we are blessed with these gifts, we are empowered to make a difference for others around us by *selling* the story of Jesus through how we live and through sharing these things. The more we individually and together as the Church use our time, talents, and treasures for the sake of helping others, the easier it is to carry out the mission of the Church to *make disciples* by sharing the love of Jesus.

In this wrestling match of faith and life, because of the death and resurrection of Jesus, the result is scripted, the victory is ours, and the ending is happy. How we get to the end of the match is ours to write and tell. There will be times in our lives where there will be pain as we wrestle with the pain and struggle that sin brings. It may sometimes feel as if we are going to lose the match. But we can always be confident of this: God knows the ending of our story and, our hands will be raised in victory!

Chapter 22
Thy Will be Done

I rolled out of the CAT scan machine and looked up at the doctor. I asked, "Am I going to die?" thinking that it would jokingly take some of the tension out of the air. In all seriousness he responded by saying, "You are if we don't take you for surgery right now." As they quickly rolled me into the operating room, I could only find myself repeatedly saying, "Thy will be done..."

There have been two scary moments in my life when I have stared death in the eye and faced my own frailty and mortality as a human being. The first was the moment above on April 5, 1994. It was two days after Easter Sunday. It was my first Easter Sunday as a pastoral intern at the Our Redeemer Lutheran Church in Aquebogue.

After the intensity of Holy Week and a successful Easter Sunday, a member of the church with whom I had built a friendship said, "let's go up to Loon Mountain in New Hampshire for a day of spring skiing." I took him up on the offer and the two of us drove the six hours from Riverhead, New York, to Lincoln, New Hampshire.

We arrived late Monday afternoon. We had some dinner and then took in the final game of the NCAA men's basketball tournament. We went to bed early, intending to get up at sunrise to catch the first tracks in the snow on that Tuesday morning. It was a glorious, beautiful day. We were among the first down the trails and enjoyed a few hours of nearly empty slopes.

As it neared lunch time, on the last run we were going to take before we retired to the ski lodge for some food, I fell face first into the snow. I landed awkwardly with my hand under my stomach and the force of the fall knocked the wind out of me. I had taken some much worse and more painful falls during my few skiing adventures, so I didn't think anything serious about this fall. After a moment or two, I got back up and skied down the rest of the mountain and we headed to the lodge for some lunch.

Just as I was enjoying the first few bites of my delicious medium-rare hamburger, I passed out, mid-sentence, and face planted into my lunch plate. When I came to a few minutes later, I was headed toward an ambulance and on my way to the hospital.

During the ambulance ride, my blood pressure kept bottoming out, and I would periodically lose consciousness. It was clear to the medical professionals that something was going on internally, but they could not pinpoint the exact problem.

Within minutes of my arrival at the hospital I was whisked into an emergency CAT scan and learned through my encounter with the doctor, as I was rolled out of the machine, that I had serious internal bleeding. They still could not determine where the bleeding was coming from, and they needed to get inside my stomach as soon as possible.

During the long, agonizing roll through the hallways to the surgical suite, I could only keep repeating "Thy will be done" as I thought about my wife and Harrison, not even two years old, who were still back on Long Island, and at this point, had no idea what was going on. This was before the popularity of cell phones. If you were not home to receive a call, then you didn't know what was going on. In those few moments before they knocked me out, I could only think about what would become of them and the church if I died.

As it turned out, my spleen had ruptured from my fall. The surgeon reported that my spleen was enlarged, contributing to the ease with which it tore. I had mononucleosis during college and an enlarged spleen can sometimes linger in its aftermath. As a token and reminder of this life and death experience, I wear a twelve-inch scar down the center of my stomach.

It would take me another ten years before I would hit the ski slopes again.

Twenty-one years after that moment, I again had to face the reality that I was not invincible. On Monday, August 23, 2015, Lisa and I traveled into Manhattan to spend an afternoon visiting with Samantha, who had moved into the city. Later that evening we were going to Brooklyn to see the professional wrestling show SummerSlam®.

During our afternoon together with Samantha and Hunter, who also joined us, we decided to take a walk in the Highline Park on Manhattan's west side. The park is a converted railroad line that has been beautifully redeveloped as a one and half mile nature walk. The rail line formerly supplied the beef that was processed in the meat-packing district of the city.

There are two flights of stairs to reach the elevated rail line and enter the park. By the time I climbed the two flights of steps I was so out of breath that I had to sit down for several minutes. This was not good, and I was scared. I had just taken a jog and gone to the gym earlier that weekend, so it made no sense to me why I would be so winded. I knew something was wrong.

On our way home from the city the next day, we stopped

at my primary care doctor, who immediately informed me that my heart was out of rhythm. He made arrangements for me to see a cardiologist the next day.

Upon first visiting with the cardiologist, before the echocardiogram was performed, he informed me that I was experiencing an episode of atrial fibrillation (Afib) and that it was not something to be too concerned about. In his professional opinion, it could be easily remedied and controlled.

But when I returned to his office after the echocardiogram, the mood and the atmosphere in the doctor's office changed dramatically. As I sat down in front of his desk, the doctor first asked if I was a drug addict. I told him that I have never taken any illegal drugs in my life. I have never even puffed some marijuana. He then asked if I took steroids. I would have taken that as a compliment, if the situation hadn't been so unnerving.

He finally came out with it and told me that my heart was seriously enlarged and damaged. My ejection fraction, which is the strength with which the heart pumps blood through the body, was around fourteen percent. A normal, healthy ejection fraction should be above sixty-five percent. He finished the visit by encouraging me to get my things in order, implying that I did not have long to live.

To say that I was shocked and angry would not adequately capture the chaotic conflict of thoughts and questions shooting around my head. "How could I have a bad heart at forty-five years old?" The whole reason I jogged, which I never really enjoyed or looked forward to, was to have a strong and healthy heart. I tried to eat foods that had the "heart healthy" label on them like oatmeal and other less-than-exciting and tasteless foods. This made absolutely no sense to me! I was angry and starting to reason with God. "What is this God, some sort of delayed punishment for my divorce and the mess my life had formerly become?" But that made no sense either. My life was back on track, and I know that's not how God works. I was enjoying my service to the people at St. Paul's, East Northport. My thoughts went to Lisa and then to the children. Though they were basically adults, the job wasn't done yet. My ex-wife was still struggling, especially in her relationship with our children. Therefore, they still needed me.

On the way home from the doctor's office, Lisa and I sat in a diner and ate a slice of cake. "Why not?" I thought to myself; my heart was already broken. Why try anymore?! We talked seriously about the possible outcomes of this. I told her that "It is what it is" and I'm ok if this is the end of the line. We then talked about the children and what we would share with them about the situation.

A few weeks later, after getting some discreet advice from a member of St. Paul's, who was a doctor, I was referred to one of the most respected electrophysiologists on Long Island. Fortunately, he was not so doom and gloom about the situation. He had complete confidence that he would not only be able to get my heart back in rhythm but also repair the damage.

It was a miracle that I did not have a stroke or cardiac event before I discovered the AFib. I was probably out of rhythm for weeks, if not months, before it got so bad that I couldn't breathe. In the meantime, I kept running and going to the gym. A disaster was in the making. In the aftermath of this health discovery, I took up walking instead of running. But the effects were not the same; and for a time, while I was wrestling to get this under control, my weight slowly crept up higher than I liked.

The journey to full recovery and overcoming this issue has taken years and is ongoing. I have been zapped with the paddles to put my heart back in rhythm more times than I care to remember. I have undergone three ablations. An ablation is when the doctor goes into the heart surgically and freezes or burns tissue on the heart to redirect the electrical current that messes up causing the heart to go out of rhythm. For years I have had to take a pill twice a day to keep me in rhythm.

As we searched for possible contributing factors to this issue, it appeared that anytime I drank alcohol, beyond one or two drinks, my heart went out of rhythm. Therefore, if I wanted to live a longer life and be around for my family, I had to make the decision to completely eliminate drinking alcohol from my life. Having a job that is very social in nature, where I am called to visit people during dinner parties, attend social events like fundraisers, and say the prayer at wedding receptions, made removing the drinking of alcohol from my life no easy task.

In the year that I was born, my grandfather on my father's side, the first Harry Schenkel (I am the third) died of a heart attack while driving his car on the road at age fifty-two. I don't remember meeting him because I was only a few months old. But my Aunt Carolee tells me that I would have liked him and that we have very similar personalities. He also deeply loved Christmas. His favorite hymn, "O Little Town of Bethlehem," was sung at his funeral, even though it was October.

As I have gone through this experience, I have often wondered if he suffered from something like my heart condition that led to that fateful moment. I have been amazed and deeply thankful for the incredible awe-inspiring medical advancements that have enabled me to be healed and return to a fully normal and healthy life, albeit without alcohol. I have pondered the question "Whatever caused someone to think to run an electrical current through a human to get their heart straight?" I have been amazed at how many instruments could fit through the arteries of my leg to repair the damage. In days past, before all those marvelous medical miracles, someone with my condition would have slowly faded away as the heart got weaker and weaker from erratically beating.

Believe it or not, both of these near-death experiences have made me a better pastor. They have made me more compassionate and appreciative of the medical community. They have reminded me why my job still matters and is still important. These experiences have caused me to truly understand what is meant when we pray in the Lord's Prayer, "Thy will be done." When it comes to death, we have very little control over our lives. It is in those last moments of our lives that we are truly taking the last step of faith. It's in the hands of God, and it's up to God's will.

Through the years, I have jokingly said to parishioners, "If people stop dying, the church is out of business." But the Biblical reality is that death is the real, permanent result of life in this sin-filled, broken world. From the condemnation pronounced upon Adam and Eve after their disobedience in the Garden of Eden to the reminder from Paul in the New Testament that the "wages of sin is death," as much as we may try to avoid it, as much as we exercise and eat right, as much as we go to a plastic surgeon to slow down the march of time, and as much as we try to outlaw our demise with restrictions during pandemics, death is in all of our futures. And that's why it's so important that the church be a safe, welcoming place. For the sanctuary of the church is the only place in this world where a true and lasting answer to death is given. That answer is what the resurrection of Jesus is all about.

Chapter 23
Yet Through the Rain, The *Son* Shines

During the first week of August 2016, I was scheduled to travel to Chicago for the third weeklong session of an educational program for pastors of larger churches. A couple of days before the trip, I received word from my Aunt Carolee that my Uncle Bill had taken a turn for the worse. I immediately cancelled my trip to Chicago and made plans to go to Sedona, Arizona.

Less than two years earlier, in the early hours of Tuesday, September 23, 2014, Lisa's father died unexpectedly from cardiac arrest. As we were all gathered at my mother-in-law's house mourning the loss of Lisa's father, I received word from my Uncle Bill that he had just been diagnosed with stage four cancer that spread to his brain. What had started as a mere numbness and loss of strength in his hand had snowballed into a life-threatening disease.

My Uncle Bill fought valiantly for the next two years. But, as we have already discussed, nobody escapes death. Two mornings before he died, my Aunt Carolee had to break the news to my Uncle Bill that he would no longer be going for his chemotherapy treatments. In the hours that followed, we each had a chance to share our final goodbyes with him and to tell him what he meant to our lives. I was blessed with the privilege of thanking him for being the strong male integrity-filled role model that was so desperately missing from my life.

As we shared these sentiments with him, it was, appropriately, raining outside. But as we finished those thoughts, I noticed that even though it was raining, the sun was still shining through. A few days later, those words "Yet through the rain, the sun shines" would become the title for the sermon that I would preach for Uncle Bill's funeral.

The Gospel lesson that I preached from during his funeral is the same Gospel lesson that I used when I preached at the funeral for Lisa's father. The Gospel lesson is my favorite chapter in the Bible. It's a passage that I feel says the most about who our Savior really is. It is the Gospel lesson that one day, will be read at my own funeral.

I share here the Gospel reading from John 11:1-44 (NRSV):

> Now a certain man was ill, Lazarus of Bethany, the village of Mary and her sister Martha. ²Mary was the one who anointed the Lord with perfume and wiped his feet with her hair; her brother Lazarus was ill. ³So the sisters sent a message to Jesus, "Lord, he whom you love is ill." ⁴But when Jesus heard it, he said, "This illness does not lead to death; rather it is for God's glory, so that the Son of God may be glorified through it." ⁵Accordingly, though Jesus loved Martha and her sister and Lazarus, ⁶after having heard that Lazarus was ill, he stayed two days longer in the place where he was.
> ⁷Then after this he said to the disciples, "Let us go to Judea again." ⁸The disciples said to him, "Rabbi, the Jews were just now trying to stone you, and are you going there again?" ⁹Jesus answered, "Are there not twelve hours of daylight? Those who walk during the day do not stumble, because they see the light of this

world. [10]But those who walk at night stumble, because the light is not in them." [11]After saying this, he told them, "Our friend Lazarus has fallen asleep, but I am going there to awaken him." [12]The disciples said to him, "Lord, if he has fallen asleep, he will be all right." [13]Jesus, however, had been speaking about his death, but they thought that he was referring merely to sleep. [14]Then Jesus told them plainly, "Lazarus is dead. [15]For your sake I am glad I was not there, so that you may believe. But let us go to him." [16]Thomas, who was called the Twin, said to his fellow disciples, "Let us also go, that we may die with him."

[17]When Jesus arrived, he found that Lazarus had already been in the tomb four days. [18]Now Bethany was near Jerusalem, some two miles away, [19]and many of the Jews had come to Martha and Mary to console them about their brother. [20]When Martha heard that Jesus was coming, she went and met him, while Mary stayed at home. [21]Martha said to Jesus, "Lord, if you had been here, my brother would not have died. [22]But even now I know that God will give you whatever you ask of him." [23]Jesus said to her, "Your brother will rise again." [24]Martha said to him, "I know that he will rise again in the resurrection on the last day." [25]Jesus said to her, "I am the resurrection and the life. Those who believe in me, even though they die, will live, [26]and everyone who lives and believes in me will never die. Do you believe this?" [27]She said to him, "Yes, Lord, I believe that you are the

Messiah, the Son of God, the one coming into the world."

[28]When she had said this, she went back and called her sister Mary, and told her privately, "The Teacher is here and is calling for you." [29]And when she heard it, she got up quickly and went to him. [30]Now Jesus had not yet come to the village, but was still at the place where Martha had met him. [31]The Jews who were with her in the house, consoling her, saw Mary get up quickly and go out. They followed her because they thought that she was going to the tomb to weep there. [32]When Mary came where Jesus was and saw him, she knelt at his feet and said to him, "Lord, if you had been here, my brother would not have died." [33]When Jesus saw her weeping, and the Jews who came with her also weeping, he was greatly disturbed in spirit and deeply moved. [34]He said, "Where have you laid him?" They said to him, "Lord, come and see." [35]Jesus began to weep. [36]So the Jews said, "See how he loved him!" [37]But some of them said, "Could not he who opened the eyes of the blind man have kept this man from dying?"

[38]Then Jesus, again greatly disturbed, came to the tomb. It was a cave, and a stone was lying against it. [39]Jesus said, "Take away the stone." Martha, the sister of the dead man, said to him, "Lord, already there is a stench because he has been dead four days." [40]Jesus said to her, "Did I not tell you that if you believed, you would see the glory of God?" [41]So they took away the stone. And Jesus looked upward and said, "Father, I thank

you for having heard me. [42]I knew that you always hear me, but I have said this for the sake of the crowd standing here, so that they may believe that you sent me." [43]When he had said this, he cried with a loud voice, "Lazarus, come out!" [44]The dead man came out, his hands and feet bound with strips of cloth, and his face wrapped in a cloth. Jesus said to them, "Unbind him, and let him go."

My reasons for loving this passage are abundant. In the characters that surround Jesus on his way to Lazarus' tomb, we can find each of ourselves at the various stages of faith (or lack thereof) that we experience when the pains and hard-felt effects of this sinful broken world touch us personally.

The disciples with Jesus at the time that he learns of Lazarus' illness are those faithful Bible students who want to have the right answer, who always want to do what is pleasing to God but find their own imperfection getting in the way. Jesus plainly explains to them what is going on. He tells them that Lazarus is dead and that He will be traveling there to raise him from the grave. But those disciples are too clouded by their own preconceptions and lack of understanding. They cannot hear and comprehend what Jesus is telling them. Out of blind devotion, they go along with him for the ride. They declare their loyalty by saying that they are willing to die with him.

Upon finally arriving at the home of Mary and Martha, Jesus encounters two devastated and distraught sisters. Martha is the first to confront Jesus. She comes out and declares, "Lord, if you had been here, my brother would not have died." Without hearing the tone in which Martha speaks the words, it's difficult to fully interpret the intent behind her words. She could be speaking out of great faith and trust in Jesus, honoring the power that she sees in Jesus when He does miraculous things. But I don't think that is her tone. I believe that when she speaks those words, she is angry.

She and her sister sent word to Jesus that Lazarus was ill. They had witnessed him cleanse the diseased skin of lepers. They knew He restored sight to those who were blind. They watched those who could not walk take steps again. I'm sure that when they sent for Jesus it was their prayer for healing. The unspoken implication was probably some prayer like, "Lord Jesus, we know and have seen you do these great things, now come and do the same thing for your dear friend Lazarus."

But, for Divine reasons, not known to the disciples or the sisters at that time, Jesus did not immediately run to them and answer their prayer. By the time he arrives, Lazarus is long dead, and I wouldn't blame Martha and then Mary for being angry with Him. I know that I have been there myself. How often have you prayed for something and felt that God was taking His time in answering or just ignoring your request?

Seemingly then, Martha catches herself and realizes whom she is talking to. She quickly follows up her words of anger by declaring, "But even now I know that God will give you whatever you ask of him." I believe that she is saving face here and taking a step back from her prior words of anger. She still remembers that Jesus is special and can still do something. So, she settles down a bit.

Jesus then engages her in a back-and-forth conversation about who He truly is and what He has told her about what He will do. Martha's answers to the questions are the type of answers that a politician on the stump gives to hard questions that they really don't want to answer. It culminates in Jesus saying to her, "I am the resurrection and the life. Those who believe in me, even though they die, will live, and everyone who lives and believes in me will never die. Do you believe this?" To which Martha safely answers the question with the answer that most first century Jews, looking for the Messiah, would have answered with, "Yes, Lord, I believe that you are the Messiah, the Son of God, the one coming into the world." Before Jesus' death and resurrection, a first century Jew believed that the Messiah would be one to lead them to be a great nation on earth. They were not looking for a Savior that would lead them to be the eternal nation.

Martha doesn't fully understand what she is answering but is going along with Jesus because she knows that it is the right thing to do. How often do we do that when it comes to our faith and following Jesus? We may not fully get everything the Bible tells us. We may not even completely trust the promises that are written. Yet, we continue to practice our faith because it feels like the right thing to do.

How can I be sure about this? Because later in the story, when Jesus goes to Lazarus' tomb and orders the stone to be rolled away, it is Martha who argues with him. "Lord, already there is a stench because he has been dead four days." The farthest thing from Martha's mind is that Lazarus will walk out alive a few moments after she speaks those words.

On his way to the tomb, Jesus encounters the people in the crowds. In particular are those people who are critical and skeptical of Jesus and who he is. Snidely they mock Him saying, "Could not he who opened the eyes of the blind man have kept this man from dying?" These are all the voices in our world today who are constantly questioning, undermining, and persecuting the Christian faith.

After a similar encounter with Martha's sister, Mary, Jesus arrives at the tomb and upon seeing the deep sorrow and pain that Lazarus' death has caused, we hear that Jesus does something that in my opinion teaches us the most important things that we need to know about God. One of the shortest verses in the Bible tells us the most about the heart of God – "Jesus wept."

Jesus is not weeping because He will not see Lazarus again. He already said to His disciples that He was going to Judea to raise Him again. He knows what He is going to do, and He knows that He has the power to do it. So why is Jesus crying? He is crying because another one of His dear friends has experienced the pain and the darkness that sin and death bring into the world.

What that means for us is that, as Jesus's adopted children and friends, Jesus weeps with us! When we are sitting in a chair next to the hospital bed of someone we deeply love who is dying, Jesus is crying with us. When we are looking at the casket of a lifelong partner, Jesus is weeping with us. When we are sitting alone on our bed, hardly capable of standing up because we are contemplating the worth and place of our life, Jesus's tears are flowing on our behalf.

The most important and blessed message that the Bible brings to us is that God gets us and understands us, especially when we are hurting and in pain. The heart of the Biblical message, which is the whole reason why Christmas, Good Friday, and Easter are the foundational moments of our faith, is that God is not far off. God has become incarnate. He has come near to us as a human being and He knows the pain and the sorrow that sin inflicts upon our lives.

When Jesus cries with us and for us, He is moved to action. His tears at the tomb of Lazarus led to His powerful words, "Lazarus, come out!" His tears for us lead Jesus to action for us through the sanctuary of the church. When we gather in the church, Jesus speaks to us, telling us to rise up from our tears. Jesus touches us personally, as He touched Lazarus, through the waters of Baptism and the Bread and Wine of Holy Communion.

The most beautiful part of the story is that it is all about Jesus and what Jesus is doing. The bumbling blind yet ill-informed devotion of the disciples does not deter Jesus from what He needs to do. The anger and stark emotions of Mary and Martha do not stop Jesus from staying on the path to be the answer to death. The cynical and obnoxious taunts of the crowd do not alter Jesus' intention to show that He is more powerful than it all. That's what the grace of God is all about.

If Jesus' actions at Lazarus' death were going to be determined by the level of faith and response of the those around Him as He traveled to the tomb, then He would have never commanded that the stone be rolled away. If Jesus' rising from the dead and saving us were dependent upon our faithful and holy living, heaven would be a very empty place. But fortunately for all of us, Jesus does what He does to love and save us, in spite of us. He does it because we need all the hope, all the healing, and all the love that He gives.

Our lives will never be lacking storms and events that cause us to weep. That's the sad reality of this broken, imperfect, sin-filled world. Yet, through the rain, the *Son* shines. We find shelter and safety in the midst of those storms, both those self-inflicted and those outside our control, in the sanctuary of the church.

Epilogue
F'd Up Blended Family

As Lisa and I navigated the life of blending a family, we often found ourselves humored and amazed by the manner in which Harrison, Samantha, Mackenzie, and Hunter rolled with the ups and downs and the drama and complications that come when families come apart and then reconstitute. At different times along the way, the children were encouraged and supported to pursue the counseling needed to help them sort through the emotions and situations that they were dealing with.

Through this process, they came to more fully understand that life is not perfect. Parents are not perfect. Pastors are not perfect. They are not perfect and will not live perfect lives. Their ability to grasp this came home to us in a humorous and powerful way.

One day I looked at the family's text group on my phone. One of the four children renamed the group, which included all six of us, the "f'd up blended family." They, however, had spelled out the F word in its entirety. Hey, what can I say? This is a raw and real look at my life.

Upon seeing the new title for the group, not only did I laugh and call it out to Lisa, but we both actually sighed a breath of relief. The brutal honesty that is captured in the title of our text group is a testimony to the work we have all done and God's grace in getting us to where we are today.

As vulgar as that phrase may be, I feel that it is a beautiful summation of the church. The Christian Church, on her best day, is still a f'd up blended family. We are all broken sinners who need to find and feel our place with God. Through the gifts that Jesus offers in the church and the imperfect servants called to administer them, God welcomes His f'd up children, from all backgrounds and places, to be a blessed blended family.

As time has gone on, as a tribute to the progress that we have made, I have changed the title of our family text group to "somewhat functional blended family." Through the gracious guiding hand of God, working through His Church of all denominations throughout the world, the body of Christ keeps moving forward to get somewhat more functional until that day of the Resurrection when all the dysfunction will be cast away forever. Until that day, the Church will be our sanctuary.

ABOUT THE AUTHOR

Harry Schenkel serves as pastor of St. Stephen Lutheran Church, Longwood, Florida. Prior to his call to St. Stephen in February 2021, Pastor Schenkel served various congregations and ministries from Manhattan, New York to the East End of Long Island. Additionally, he has served in roles for the larger church body, the Evangelical Lutheran Church in America. Currently, Pastor Schenkel sits on the Board of Long Island Lutheran Middle and High School, Brookville, New York. Harry also serves as the Dean of the Heart of Florida Conference of the Florida-Bahamas Synod ELCA, overseeing fifteen churches in the Orlando area.

Harry is married to Lisa, an artist working her dream job at Disney World®. Together they have four adult children. Samantha, married to Patrick, lives four miles from her parents in Florida. Harrison, Mackenzie, and Hunter still live and work in New York. Most joyfully, Harry and Lisa are awaiting the birth of their first grandchild, a boy due around Thanksgiving 2024.

Harry enjoys rooting for the NY Yankees, reading, exercising, camping, playing golf (not well), and bowling. In November 1993, Harry bowled a perfect game.

ACKNOWLEDGMENTS

Thanks to all the people whom God has called me to serve in various churches and ministries over the last thirty years, most especially the people at St. John's, Sayville, New York, St. Paul's, East Northport, New York, and my current congregation, St. Stephen, Longwood, Florida. I have been served as much by you as I have sought to serve you. Thank you also to all the pastors who have loved, taught me, and worked with me over the years. You are the unsung heroes of this book.

Thank you to Carolyn Lea and Carolyn Boswell for their limitless patience in editing my love of commas and exclamation points, which every preacher loves to abuse. This project would have never happened without the wisdom, encouragement, and expertise of Dennis McClellan.

Thank you to all who read the manuscript along the way making me feel like I was on the right path. Special thanks to Pastor Jonathan for being my friend.

Most especially, thank you to my f'd up blended family. My parents who did the best they could with what they had to work with. In spite of the deep dysfunction, they did something right by making sure the sanctuary of the church was prominent in my life. My aunt, Carolee Bruder, and prior to his death, Uncle Bill, for making up the difference from my parents. Thank you to Harrison, Samantha, Mackenzie, and Hunter for playing starring roles in my life and book. And of course, Lisa, my wife and soulmate, who has been writing this book with me for many years before pen even touched paper.

Made in the USA
Las Vegas, NV
16 October 2024

96983697R10122